TREATMENT
OF PERINATAL
MOOD DISORDERS

TREATMENT OF PERINATAL MOOD DISORDERS

NAN NELSON, MD

PERINATAL PSYCHIATRIST

To order additional copies of this book, contact:
Xlibris
1-888-795-4274
www.Xlibris.com
Orders@Xlibris.com
734490

Dedicated to Dr. Miriam Rosenthal, my mentor, my teacher,
my friend in treating women's mental health.

Special thanks to Dr. Christine Traxler for her
help in making this book possible.

CONTENTS

CONTENTS

Introduction

WHY I MAY HURT MY BABY

In medical school, we were taught first to do no harm. While studying in obstetrics, we were basically told to not interfere with the natural process of pregnancy and delivery and that nature would run its course. Let the obstetrician add medication because they knew the most. In the world of defensive medicine, why would you add medication during pregnancy? The malpractice insurance for OB/GYNs is astronomical. Women have been delivering babies since the beginning of time, and it will all turn out okay. As an intern, I was terrified of killing someone. I would check and recheck my work to make sure that I did not harm anybody. So the noninterference of medication use during pregnancy and postpartum made sense to me. As a child psychiatrist, I would interview mothers, fathers, children or adolescents, and anyone else in the nuclear family. Often, I noticed how depressed the mother was and would say to her that she is the head of the ship, and if she goes under, everyone will be in big trouble. I felt I needed to treat the mother, but because of agency regulations, I was not allowed to and would refer her to someone else whom she may or may not have followed up on. Often, I was evaluating families and the mother was pregnant again, I began to see her depression affecting both her current pregnancy and the child I was treating. I ultimately decided that if I wanted to make a difference for children I needed to help women during this vulnerable period of time during pregnancy postpartum and with lactation. What I found is that women and mothers do not take care of themselves. They'll do anything for their kids, their husband, their lover, their family, and even the PTA and church, but they put themselves last on the list of people who need help. They tell me the medications are too expensive, yet if asked if they would pay for a medication that cost as much for their child, they would say absolutely. They make sure everyone else eats three meals a day, but they rarely do. The kids would be in bed asleep, and they would clean the house, pay the bills, and complete all the things they couldn't get done during the day at their own physical and mental expense. Women are trained to take care of others. In toddlerhood, they say go take this to Daddy or Grandma or whoever, but would they ask that of their sons? Women cook meals, do the laundry, clean, check on children's homework, and make sure that everyone has bathed, slept, and eaten and has meals for school/work. They get done what needs to be done for everyone to go forward. Women in general are not taught that if they don't take care of themselves, who will? Mothers, grandmothers, cousins, coworkers, pastors, ladies at the church/temple, nurses, teachers, and even doctors tell women they should not take any medications while they are pregnant. So if they're on medication and they discover that they are pregnant, they go off them. Women tell me things that they don't tell their doctors. I often ask them if they have told their doctor, and they just look down, as if ashamed or embarrassed, and say no. When I ask why not, they say that they don't want to look weak or hysterical or be a burden to the person who helped them through their pregnancy and delivery. Here is a partial list of things that women have told me:

I can't touch the baby.

I don't feel anything. There must be something wrong with me. All the other mothers look like they're in love, but I'm not.

I wasn't made to be a mother. I don't feel anything.

Sometimes I feel like I'm in a movie. Everything feels unreal. I'm a robot.

I get so anxious. My heart beats so fast, I think I'm dying. I'm afraid I will drop her, so I change her on the floor because I can't go upstairs with her.

Everyone else can make her stop crying, but me. I must be a bad mother.

I can't sleep. I feed the baby which takes about an hour, change her, and think I'll have to be back up in thirty minutes to an hour. Why bother. So I get up and do the things that won't get done unless I do them, you know taking out the trash, cleaning the dishes... there's endless loads of laundry. Next thing you know, it's time to feed the baby again.

When I lay down, I feel anxious. I can't go to sleep. The list of things I need to do goes round and round in my head. I worry I'm not a good enough mother. I just can't relax.

My sister should've been her mother, not me. I think of killing myself 'cause I just can't do this... The system will take care of her. She's a better mother than I am. I'm no good. I scream at the baby because she cries. I just can't take it anymore.

I couldn't be alone. I felt I had to lay the baby in the ditch at the end of the driveway. I knew I couldn't do it if there was somebody else there.

I'm afraid I think I'm crazy, and they will take away the baby.

Can you tell my other kid over there in the corner to be quiet? She's gonna wake up the baby. It's weird. I know my daughters are at home, but I can see her over there in the corner, and she's making noise. I want to tell, but anybody can think I'm nuts. Am I crazy? Maybe if I just ignore it, it'll go away. Tell her to just be quiet.

I am so angry at my husband. He gets to sleep and eat. Then he comes home, and he wants me to do everything. I haven't slept, I haven't eaten, I haven't taken a shower, and all I've done is take care of that screaming baby. Then he wants sex. The last thing on earth I want is to get pregnant again.

What if I never get better?

My husband leaves; I just sit and cry. It's like I can't move. I can't breast-feed. I feel like I have no energy.

I thought of putting my thumb through that soft spot on his head (the fontanelle). I knew it was illogical, but I still thought about doing it. I didn't do it.

I'd lock myself in my room because I thought of throwing the baby against the wall when he cried.

I thought of jumping off the balcony. If I was dead, so was the baby. At least I'd have the baby when I was in hell. And we'd both feel nothing.

I'm worried the hospital gave me the wrong baby. I'm afraid to love this baby because someone will come and get her because they made a mistake. How do I know she's mine? I try to pretend she is, but there is always the question inside my mind. What if she someone else's baby.

How long do I have to stay on these medicines?

My sister had a baby. She didn't act this way. What's is wrong with me?

The baby's in the NICU. What did I do wrong? It must be my fault. I think of every cigarette I smoked during the pregnancy. It's my fault. One time, I got sick, and I took medicine. It's my fault.

My husband tells me it's my fault. If I would just relax and not be so anxious, this baby wouldn't be so irritable and cry all the time. I don't know how to relax.

It takes so much work to get out of this house. By the time you pack up the diaper bag, get the carrier, get the kids in the car, I'm exhausted. Then I feel trapped in the house.

Maybe I'm crazy, just stupid, a bad mom, I don't deserve them...

I'm afraid to take a bath. I'm afraid someone will drop an electrical cord in, and me and my baby will be electrocuted/fried.

My doctor told me to take a warm bath to relax, but I'm afraid it will boil the baby, so I didn't.

I saw on TV where a mother put her baby in the microwave. I couldn't stand the thought. So I took the microwave out of the wall and put it at the side of the road for the trash pick-up.

My energy was so high. When I couldn't sleep, I would run on the treadmill, hoping I would finally get tired and sleep.

I thought, what if I cut the baby? Then I thought, what kind of mother am I? I took out all the knives out of the kitchen, and I wouldn't let any of the kids in the kitchen. What kind of woman am I?

Every time my husband leaves the house, I'm worried he's not coming back.

My mother-in-law is driving me crazy. She wants to hold the baby all the time. What I really need is for her to do something. It's my baby. I dread seeing her car pull in the driveway. My husband says I'm making this all up. He tells me, just get over it.

What's wrong with me? Other women seem to do this.

I have not slept at all in 48 hours or more.

I do not feel loving toward my baby and can't even go through the motions to take care of him/her.

I am afraid I might harm myself in order to escape this pain.

I am afraid I might actually do something to hurt the baby.

I hear sounds or voices when no one is around.

I feel that my thoughts are not my own or that they are totally out of my control.

I have lost a lot of weight without trying to

I feel like such a bad mother.

Maybe I should have never become a mother. I think I may have made a mistake.

Chapter 1

INTRODUCTION

*There is no perfect decision, and no decision is risk free. Patients
need to know about the risk of exposure to medications and
they need to know about the risk of untreated disease.*

—Dr. Lee Cohen, University of Iowa, Neuropsychiatry Reviews, *June 2001*

Twenty percent of women and 10 percent of men around the world experience
clinical depression. While most people believe that pregnancy is relatively
protective against mental illness, recent research has indicated that up to 20
percent of pregnant women suffer from some type of anxiety or mood disorder
during their pregnancy (1). One out of every eight to ten postpartum mothers or
four hundred thousand per year reportedly have postpartum depression (PPD).
According to the American Academy of Pediatricians, eight hundred thousand
US women suffer postpartum depression. This is a misunderstood, misdiagnosed,
and mistreated diagnosis and an underdiagnosed obstetrical complication, and an
estimated 50 percent of cases go undetected. Every woman who gets pregnant is
at risk of having a mood disorder.

"Postpartum psychosis is a qualitatively different illness from postpartum
depression and strikes one out of every 1,000 deliveries," explains Dr. Emily
Dossett, a reproductive psychiatrist and assistant clinical professor at the Los
Angeles County-University of Southern California Maternal Wellness Clinic.
She also serves as the reproductive psychiatrist on California's Task Force on the
Status of Maternal Mental Health Care.

"Risk factors," she continues, "include a history of psychosis, bipolar disorder
and having had symptoms of mental illness in the past. Those with postpartum

1

psychosis are at a substantially increased risk of committing suicide and/or infanticide. These acts are the result of devastating biological disorders, not a conscious choice. But with proper diagnosis and intervention, there is recovery and tragedies tied to untreated psychosis can be avoided."

Dr. Dossett adds, "Screening and treatment efforts have not targeted postpartum psychosis. Recommendations such as those issued by the United States Preventative Services Task Force (USPSTF) will raise awareness about maternal mental health disorders overall and help health-care providers begin a dialog about mental health with their patients."

This is an epidemiological report of postpartum episodes. It's an older study, but it shows the clear spike of psychiatric hospitalizations around the delivery of infants.

Epidemiology of Postpartum Episodes

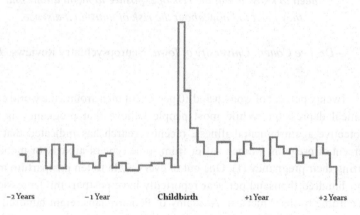

Kendell RE et al. *Br J Psychiatry.* 1987;150:662-673.

Those who are at the highest risk include women who have had a history of a prior psychiatric disorder and who have stopped taking their psychotropic medications because they have been found to be pregnant.

In a recent study (3), a group of eighty-two women who maintained their antidepressant medication during their pregnancy suffered a rate of 26 percent relapse compared with the 68 percent relapse rate in women who stopped taking their antidepressant. In the study, it was estimated that those who stopped taking their medication were five times more likely to suffer from a relapse compared with women who continued their antidepressant therapy. Elevated rates of relapse of mental illness were also seen in women who carried the diagnosis of bipolar disorder.

In another study (3), about 71 percent of women had at least one episode of mood-disordered symptoms. Those who stopped their mood stabilizers suffered a relapse rate of 86 percent compared with a relapse rate of only 37 percent in women who chose to stay on their mood stabilizer.

Although there has been limited data gathered over the last thirty years on pregnant women and psychotropic medication, evidence suggest that certain medications are safe during pregnancy. The data, however, are not complete. For this reason, many women choose to stop taking their psychotropic medication during pregnancy or opt for no medical treatment if diagnosed for the first time in their pregnancy.

Problems with the US FDA Category Designations as They Apply to Pregnancy

The US Food and Drug Administration (FDA) developed guidelines in 1975 that outlined the safety of various medications used in pregnancy. All medications are assigned a letter ranking according to their safety profile as evidenced by research on the drug in pregnancy. The pregnancy categories are as follows (4):

- Category A. There have been well-controlled studies done that have demonstrated no risk to the fetus in the first or later trimesters of pregnancy. Examples include folic acid, magnesium sulfate, levothyroxine, and triiodothyronine.
- Category B. There have been animal studies on pregnant animals which showed no risk to the fetus, but there are no well-controlled studies in humans. Examples include penicillin, metformin, cyclobenzaprine, and hydrochlorothiazide.
- Category C. Studies on animals have been done showing some type of adverse effect on the fetus in the absence of well-controlled human studies. The benefits of the drug may warrant its use in spite of the possibility of risk. Examples include gabapentin, amlodipine, prednisone, tramadol, and trazodone.
- Category D. There is research evidence indicating a risk to the fetus or evidence based on marketing experience in humans, but there may be potential benefits that outweigh the risks. Examples include losartan, clonazepam, lorazepam, alprazolam, and lisinopril.
- Category X. There have been studies in humans or animals showing the probability of fetal abnormalities or absolute evidence of fetal risk based on research or marketing experience on the drug. In such cases, the risks

3

are too great despite the possible benefits. Examples include simvastatin, methotrexate, warfarin, atorvastatin, and finasteride.

- Category N. The drug is not currently classified by the FDA.
- Usually, there is the necessity of only a limited degree of animal research data used to give the drug its destinations. While the above categories are in use so that doctors can make adequate decisions around prescribing a medication during pregnancy, this system has its limitations. Primarily, there are very limited human studies on these drugs, and if new data are found, they are rarely incorporated into updating the drug's initial category assignment. The risks to not treating the illness are also not part of the drug's assignment, nor is the severity of the patient's illness or the risk of recurrence of the disease.
- With psychiatric medications, most are found to be assigned to Category C or Category D, although the FDA is attempting to improve the way drugs are currently categorized, with attempts being made to give more information as to the benefits and risks of a certain medication in a more descriptive way. In the newer way to categorize drugs, there will be more information on the risks of not treating the disorder for which the medication is proposed to be used.

Looking at the Risks

Women who have had a history of some kind of psychiatric disorder often seek the advice of their obstetrician or psychiatrist as to what to do about taking psychotropic medications during their pregnancy. Some have their first episode of psychiatric disease while they are pregnant. Others have unplanned pregnancies during which time they are already taking psychotropic medications. Women often stop their psychiatric medication as soon as they determine they are pregnant; however, there are risks in doing this. Many doctors and nurses tell their patients to stop all medications.

The decision of starting or maintaining a psychotropic medication during pregnancy needs to be based on an understanding of the potential risks to the fetus as well as on the risks associated with not treating the disease in the pregnant mother. Having a psychiatric condition during pregnancy is not altogether benign so that significant morbidity can occur in both mother and fetus. For this reason, holding back or stopping the medication in pregnancy may not be the safest choice.

Both anxiety and depression in a pregnant woman have been linked to several different adverse outcomes. Women who are diagnosed with a psychiatric disorder while pregnant are less likely to get prenatal care and are more likely to use illicit drugs, cigarettes, and alcohol during pregnancy that are known to negatively impact the pregnancy.

There have been several research studies showing intrauterine growth retardation and low gestational age birthweight in babies born to mothers who suffer from depression. Women who suffer from increased distress while pregnant also carry a risk of preterm birth. In addition, things like pre-eclampsia, cesarean section, infant fetal distress, infant hypoglycemia, and premature births have been found in women who were depressed during their pregnancy.

This means that it is important for pregnant women who developed a psychiatric disease during their pregnancy to undertake a complete risk/benefit evaluation. This must include both the risks of taking the medication as well as the risks of allowing the psychiatric condition to go untreated.

Risks of Exposure to Psychiatric Medications

It's clear that all psychotropic medications cross the placental barrier, and there are no psychotropic medications currently approved for use during pregnancy by the FDA. This means that, in prescribing psychotropic drugs during pregnancy, there must be considerations about the risks of exposure to the fetus as well as the risks of not treating the disease state.

The Possibility of Fetal Birth Defects

In the United States, the risk of having a major birth defect in all pregnancies is between 2 and 5 percent. The development of the major organ systems occurs early in the first trimester and is usually completed by the twelfth week of pregnancy. This means that the risks to the fetus by taking a psychotropic medication depends on the timing of the exposure to the medication. Particular care must be taken in giving psychotropic medications during these early weeks of the first trimester. Some drugs are classified as teratogens, which are medications that interfere with the developmental process in utero and result in a malformation or dysfunction of a major organ. Each organ system develops at its own pace, and each has a critical period of time in which exposure to a teratogen can result in damage to the organ. One example of this is neural tube defects, which tend to occur if a teratogen is given to the mother within the first four weeks of pregnancy. On the other hand, the great vessels and the heart are at their greatest degree of development between four and nine weeks' gestation and are at their greatest risk of compromise during this period.

Neonatal Withdrawal Symptoms

This is also referred to as perinatal syndrome or neonatal toxicity. It involves a wide range of behavioral and physical symptoms seen in the neonate that is the direct result of exposure to a drug around the time of delivery. This area of neonatal medicine has not been well studied, but there are anecdotal reports of various types of neonatal problems as a result of acute withdrawal of a drug from the neonate's system at the time of birth. Clearly, more research needs to be done to identify these symptoms as they relate the various drugs a pregnant mother can take during the pregnancy (whether they be illicit drugs or prescription medications).

Long-Term Effects on the Infant

There is very little information on the long-term effects of giving a mother a psychotropic drug and the eventual long-term outcome in the infant. The brain especially is developing throughout pregnancy and in the years after pregnancy. For this reason, the brain is especially vulnerable to any type of toxic substance during the pregnancy. There are clear-cut effects on the neural tube, which closes at about thirty-two days after conception, but exposure to psychotropic medications after that time can have subtle effects on the subsequent CNS function and postnatal behavior that are not yet clear. When we talk of behavioral teratogenesis, we are talking about the fact that a psychotropic medication given in pregnancy may exert long-term neural and behavioral effects on the growing child. We do not yet know whether exposure to antidepressant medications in utero put a child at a later risk of developing some kind of behavioral or cognitive difficulty as they grow older. There are very few studies on this topic done in humans.

The effects of depression on maternal attitudes include guilt or anxiety about parenting, fear of not being able to love the baby, and difficulty enjoying the baby. She may interact less often with the baby, and she may be unable to soothe the baby, refusing to look at or hold the baby. She may be negative or have disinterested feelings and hostile expressions toward the baby.

One of the women I evaluated told me that her baby was butt ugly. The concern was being able to bond with this baby she could not even hold. Another woman described her baby as being evil because all she did was cry.

The effects of this on the infant and child include poor mother-infant attachment with increased irritability and lethargy or poor sleep for both the infant and the mother. Also seen are language delays, behavioral difficulties, and lower cognitive performances. Mental health disorders are more prevalent with attention problems. Babies are more withdrawn and crying all the time and have temper issues. There are often disruptions in wake-sleep cycles and feeding problems.

Untreated depression in women leads to prenatal behaviors such as poor nutrition, poor prenatal care, and substance abuse. It also leads to poor parenting behaviors. These all lead to a longer persistence of symptoms and an increased risk of postpartum depression with subsequent children. There's also an increased risk of relapse.

Existing psychological disorders prior to pregnancy either stay the same or worsen during pregnancy, especially anxiety disorders and obsessive-compulsive disorders.

Women with mental illness during pregnancy have an increased risk of preterm delivery, cesarean sections, low birth weight, and neonatal intensive care unit admissions for infants.

It will go away if I just 'tough it out'
and pretend it's not happening...

—*Pregnant woman*

Chapter 2

DEPRESSION IN PREGNANCY

While pregnancy is supposed to be a happy time in a couple's life, it can be a time of increased stress, confusion, fear, and depression. According to the American Congress of Obstetricians and Gynecologists (ACOG), about 20 percent of women suffer from some or all the symptoms of depression while they are pregnant.

Depression is a common mood disorder among women. Studies indicate that about 25 percent of all women develop depression at some point in their lives. Sometimes, this depression occurs during pregnancy. Unfortunately, depression in pregnancy is greatly underreported because many assume that the symptoms are related to a hormonal imbalance as a result of the pregnancy rather than a true mental disorder. Making this assumption can be risky not only for the mother but also for the unborn fetus.

Antepartum Depression

Antepartum depression is a mood disorder that affects a woman while she is pregnant. Changes in brain chemistry are responsible for the mood changes seen in all types of depression. While a woman is pregnant, there can be hormonal changes that affect the parts of the brain related to the development of depression. Along with the hormonal changes can come difficult situations in life that together lead to depression in pregnancy.

Causes of Depression in Pregnancy

There are some women who are at greater risk of developing depression during pregnancy. Some of the factors that play into getting depressed while pregnant include the following:

- Being of a younger age at the time a woman becomes pregnant.
- Being a sufferer of premenstrual dysphoric disorder (PMDD)
- Having a history of depression in the past
- Living by oneself or having poor support from the woman's family
- Having poor social supports
- Being a victim of domestic violence
- Suffering from marital discord during the pregnancy
- Being uncertain about being pregnant
- Taking illicit drugs during the pregnancy
- Having a family history of depression
- Having undergone fertility treatments to achieve this pregnancy
- Having a prior pregnancy loss (stillbirth or miscarriage)
- Having stressful life events during the pregnancy
- Having a history of childhood trauma
- Having complications during the pregnancy

If a woman suffers from one or several of these risk factors, it can result in chemical changes in the brain which lead to the depressive state. While this is true, women with no risk factors can still suffer from antenatal depression.

How Can Depression Affect a Pregnancy?

A depressed pregnant woman often suffers a decreased ability to care for herself. She may be less likely to follow the doctor's instructions and may fail to take prenatal vitamins and get enough sleep and has stopped eating healthy meals. All of these have a direct input into the growth and development of the fetus.

Depressed women tend to be at a greater risk of using alcohol, tobacco products, and illicit drugs, which also impact the growth and development of the fetus. Depressed women are at a greater risk of opioid abuse in pregnancy and have higher rates of fetal alcohol syndrome. A depressed woman who smokes suffers a greater chance of having a small-for-gestational-age infant and a greater risk of stillbirths. Bonding with the baby once it is born is greatly affected by the mother suffering from depression.

The stresses of being pregnant can result in depression as a new finding or the worsening of a depression that preexisted the pregnancy. The incidence of postpartum depression is considerably increased in a woman who suffers from depression during the pregnancy.

Depression that is not treated during the pregnancy not only affects a woman's ability to get and maintain adequate prenatal care and maternal/fetal nutrition but also leads to substance abuse, poor parenting behaviors once the baby is born, and postpartum depression and all that it entails. Some women have a steady progression of symptoms that lead naturally from antepartum depression to postpartum depression without a break between the two.

Women who are depressed during pregnancy suffer a greater risk of postpartum depression when they have more children, even if they don't have depression during their subsequent pregnancies. These high-risk women need careful follow-up throughout the pregnancies and in the postpartum state because they tend to repeat the same symptoms over and over again the more they become pregnant.

Untreated depression in pregnancy as well as other mental illnesses in pregnancy means the woman has a greater chance of having a preterm delivery, a low-birth-weight infant, a cesarean section, or an infant that requires care in the neonatal intensive care unit. This speaks to the need to weigh the risks of taking medication for depression against the benefits of taking medications and the risk of not treating the depression at all.

I thought of jumping off the balcony. If I was dead, so was the baby. At least I'd have the baby when I was in hell. And we'd both feel nothing.

—*Depressed pregnant woman*

Signs and Symptoms of Depression during Pregnancy

In order for the diagnosis to be made, at least some of the symptoms of depression must be present for at least two weeks during the pregnancy. Some of these signs and symptoms include the following:

- Persistent sadness that pervades much of the woman's life and goes beyond the normal bounds of being unhappy.
- Difficulty concentrating on activities of daily living.
- Failure to plan for the baby. This can include failing to buy clothing for the baby or failing to set up a nursery.

- Sleep disturbances. This can include sleeping for long periods of time or having episodes of insomnia that include difficulty getting to sleep or maintaining a full night's sleep.
- Having a loss of interest in hobbies or activities the woman used to enjoy.
- Feelings of apathy around having a baby.
- Failing to care for the body's basic needs including its nutritional needs.
- Engaging in destructive behaviors such as substance abuse, tobacco use, and alcohol abuse.
- Having recurrent thoughts of hopelessness, death, or suicide. Suicidal attempts are not out of the question in pregnancy, and this can adversely affect the baby, especially if it involves taking an overdose of medication or illicit drugs.
- Increased anxiety that can be generalized or focused around the pregnancy itself.
- Feelings of guilt or worthlessness. In pregnancy, this can mean feeling guilty about being pregnant, feeling guilty about not taking care of herself, or feeling as though she will be a poor and worthless mother.
- Ruminating over the pregnancy, such as ruminating over the health of the fetus or the health of the mother.
- Increased tearfulness.
- Lack of energy, which translates into decreased mental energy and physical energy,
- Having hallucinations or delusions, which may be related to the pregnancy or the fetus. This is usually reserved for severe cases of antenatal depression.

Nonmedication (Natural) Ways of Managing the Depressed Pregnant Woman

Mild cases of depression can be managed through things like psychotherapy and lifestyle changes. The woman should be encouraged to reduce activity that is stressful and engage more in activities she might enjoy.

There is some evidence that light therapy, often used in the treatment of seasonal affective disorder, can help a pregnant woman feel better without the use of antidepressant therapy. This involves the use of full spectrum light boxes on a daily basis to alter the brain chemistry.

Psychotherapy can help with improving the woman's level of self-care throughout the pregnancy. Close observation of her eating habits, weight, and use of harmful substances can be done under the guidance of a good psychotherapist. Relaxation techniques can be made use of in order to manage the anxiety that often goes along with the depressive symptoms. Support groups may be available for women who have depression in pregnancy or for people who are depressed in general.

Exercise can raise serotonin levels and may be enough to reduce the chances of needing to take antidepressant therapy. Most pregnant women can engage in mild to moderate exercise such as swimming, bicycling, and walking through much of the pregnancy. Such activities can be encouraged and followed by the psychotherapist.

The woman should be encouraged to have a regular sleep schedule and to get adequate rest. The depression may be so severe as to limit the ability of the woman to continue with her job. This time can be filled with support groups, more time with family, rest, and sleep.

The type of nutrition a depressed pregnant woman receives can have an impact on her symptoms. Foods that are highly processed and high in sugar and beverages that are high in caffeine can affect the woman's thought processes and other symptoms. The same is true of foods high in artificial additives. On the other hand, a balanced diet with fruits, vegetables, whole grains, and lean meats can ensure adequate fetal nutrition and a better mental outlook for the mother.

There are some studies indicating that acupuncture in pregnancy is both safe and effective in managing mild depression without the use of drugs.

Pregnant women can also relieve some of their depressive symptoms by taking mercury-free supplements containing Omega 3 fatty acids. The research on this is somewhat sparse, but it certainly can't hurt, and there is some evidence that it can help ease depression.

Herbal remedies have been suggested for the management of depression in pregnancy; however, there is little research to support the safety of herbal products in pregnancy. Some choices include St. John's Wort, SAM-e, 5-HTP, vitamin B6, and magnesium supplementation. These cannot be used along with conventional antidepressants, and the dosages of these supplements must be left to a trained herbalist who understands pregnancy and depression.

Depression in pregnancy is not uncommon and carries risks to the health of the mother and the unborn fetus. Natural remedies can be used in mild to moderate cases of antenatal depression, but if the depression is severe or associated with hallucinations or delusions, treatment with prescription antidepressants may be necessary.

How long do I have to stay on these medicines?

—Depressed pregnant woman

Chapter 3

TREATMENT OF DEPRESSION
IN PREGNANCY

Among the various antidepressants, fluoxetine (Prozac), sertraline (Zoloft), paroxetine (Paxil), and citalopram (Celexa) have been studied the most. Data on more than 2,500 women taking fluoxetine during pregnancy show no increase in congenital abnormalities in the fetuses. There has been one study on more than five hundred infants who suffered exposure to citalopram during the first trimester of pregnancy revealing no increased risk of congenital abnormality.

There have been several combined studies on exposure to selective serotonin reuptake inhibitors (SSRIs) indicating no risk of congenital defects in babies born after exposure to these drugs. The only exception to this has been paroxetine (Paxil) (5). The biggest controversy around using this drug in pregnancy includes reports that taking it in the first trimester of pregnancy was linked to heart defects, such as atrial septal defects and ventricular septal defects. For this reason, paroxetine is labeled category D in pregnancy and is not recommended for use in pregnancy.

There have been many studies looking into the risk of taking tricyclic antidepressants in pregnancy and the risk of congenital abnormalities. None of these studies showed an association with this classification of drugs and any congenital abnormalities in the fetus or newborn. Of all the tricyclic antidepressants, nortriptyline and desipramine are considered the preferred drugs because they have fewer anticholinergic side effects and are less likely to cause orthostatic hypotension that is so common among pregnant women. However, tricyclic antidepressants are lethal if taken in overdose.

Another drug studied on pregnant women has been bupropion (Wellbutrin) (6). This can be used in women who don't respond to tricyclics or fluoxetine/

SSRIs. Studies have shown no increased risk of congenital deformities when this drug is used in pregnancy. There is a Bupropion Pregnancy Registry maintained by the manufacturer showing data from more than five hundred pregnancies in which the mother was exposed to the drug during the first trimester of pregnancies. Among all these pregnancies, there were twenty congenital malformations found. This constitutes a 3.9 percent risk of malformation, consistent with what is seen in pregnant women who have had no exposure to teratogens. Bupropion does not treat anxiety, which is often a part of depression.

Another retrospective study (7) on more than 1,200 newborns who had fetal exposure to bupropion (Wellbutrin) in the first trimester showed no excess risk of congenital malformations in those infants exposed to bupropion when compared with those who were not exposed to the drug. This included heart defects.

There is little information on the safety of using monoamine oxidase inhibitors (MAOIs) in pregnancy. Partly because of this, it is rarely used in a pregnant woman. It also has the potential to produce hypertension in women who also take terbutaline or other tocolytic medications. There is also little information on the use of venlafaxine (Effexor) or duloxetine (Cymbalta) in pregnancy.

While these kinds of reports are helpful, there needs to be studies on larger groups of people in order to identify whether or not these newer antidepressant medications are safe. About five hundred to six hundred fetal exposures to a drug are required to identify a difference in the rate of congenital abnormalities over that seen in people not taking the drug. The drugs citalopram, fluoxetine, and sertraline have been studied in this way and are thus the most commonly used SSRIs in pregnancy.

There have been several recent research reports (8–11) that suggest exposure to selective serotonin reuptake inhibitors close to the time of birth may be linked to poorer infant outcomes. These studies focused on a variety of temporary neonatal distress symptoms related to withdrawal from antidepressants at the time of birth. These symptoms seem to affect nearly 25 percent of infants who had been exposed to SSRIs during the latter stages of pregnancy. The major symptoms seen have been restlessness, tremor, hypertonicity, and crying behaviors among exposed individuals. Fortunately, these symptoms seem to last only one to four days following the birth and are resolved without any type of treatment. No baby has ever died from jittery baby syndrome.

Because of these studies, it is currently recommended that women taper off the use of SSRI therapy before having their baby. Doing so, on the other hand, hasn't been found to change the outcome. The other problem is that stopping these medications puts women at a greater risk of developing postpartum depression after the birth of their child.

Another risk of taking SSRIs in later pregnancy is the risk of persistent pulmonary hypertension of the newborn (PPHN) (12). The use of SSRIs has been linked to a sixfold risk of developing PPHN in babies exposed to the drugs after the twentieth week of pregnancy. This was just one study and no other studies have shown this increase in risk.

As for the long-term effects of tricyclics and SSRIs in utero on human development, only two studies have reported on these. One study (13) examined 135 children who had an exposure to fluoxetine or tricyclic medication in pregnancy. There was no difference in temperament, IQ, mood, behavior, distractibility, or activity level when compared with children who weren't exposed to the drug. These children were followed until they reached the age of seven.

Every other mother leaves with a baby. I have nothing, I am not a mother, I didn't get to hold him, there's nothing to grieve, and it's as if nothing happened, but it did. People say you can always have another baby, I'll never have this baby again.

—Woman after miscarriage

Maternal Depression and Adverse Outcomes/Perinatal Loss

The reasons behind a woman's miscarriage, especially early events, are hard to obtain because data must be gathered after the woman recognizes that she is pregnant, which is usually after six weeks' gestation. Fetal loss after this time happens in about 8 percent of women, and large sample sizes are needed to detect differences in miscarriage with and without depression or the use of antidepressants. For this reason, there is little information on depression and the risk of miscarriage.

The baby's in utero growth is typically seen as delivering a small-for-gestational-age infant with a birth weight of less than 10 percent of the age-adjusted weight. Depressed mothers have been linked to having low birth weight and small-for-gestational-age infants in some studies (14).

Preterm delivery occurring prior to thirty-seven weeks' gestation is associated with having a depressive disorder during pregnancy, although not all studies bear this out. The data available doesn't support or refute a link between prenatal depression and preterm delivery. Fortunately, infants born to depressed mothers have no increase in congenital defects, but they have been found to have less activity, increased irritability, and fewer facial expressions compared with babies born to mothers without depression (15).

Smalls studies have shown that infants born to depressed women have physiological profiles that include increased levels of cortisol, decreased serotonin, and decreased peripheral levels of dopamine, with lower vagal tone and greater activation of the right frontal lobe on EEG (15).

Few studies have been done on the specific effects of antenatal depression on the development of older children. In general, depressive symptoms in the mother, rather than a diagnosis of maternal depression, has been the focus of most studies. In one study, exposure to maternal depression between eighteen and thirty-two weeks into the pregnancy but not after birth showed a greater degree of developmental delay at eighteen months when compared with children who had healthy mothers in pregnancy (16).

Taking Antidepressants and Birth Outcomes

More than 80 percent of women take at least one dose of some kind of medication besides vitamins during pregnancy. The use of multiple medications while pregnant makes it hard to assess the impact of just one medication on fetal outcomes. This is complicated by the fact that women who are taking an antidepressant during pregnancy are more likely to also be on another prescription medication (17). SSRIs are the most frequently prescribed class of medications. The use of tricyclics and MAOI medications is infrequent in pregnancy.

There is an increased risk of spontaneous abortion in those women who have taken certain antidepressants in early pregnancy. In one review of more than 3,500 women, the miscarriage rates were 12.4 percent for those who took antidepressants versus 8.7 percent for women who were unexposed to antidepressants (18). No differences were seen between the various antidepressants.

Growth Effects

Reductions in birth weight, including low birth weight and small-for-gestational-age infants, are associated with SSRI use in pregnancy (19). A birth registry out of Sweden revealed that low birth weight babies were associated with both tricyclic antidepressant and SSRI use, but the infants were not small for gestational age. This means that these babies were likely born early but were of normal weight for their gestational age.

The time and duration of exposure to an antidepressant must also be taken into account but are hard to determine. In many cases, third-trimester exposure means that the women took medication throughout the pregnancy rather than just in the third trimester. Those who took antidepressants in the first trimester, on the other hand, usually just took them during the first trimester. Women who need medication in the third trimester tend to have more serious underlying illnesses.

It isn't possible to say when the exposure occurred or whether or not more severe illness had a greater impact on fetal growth (20).

The rate of preterm birth (less than thirty-seven weeks' gestation) in the United States is 12.7 percent and is the leading cause of perinatal morbidity and mortality. For this reason, the relationship between antidepressant use and preterm birth is important. There has been evidence that preterm birth is linked to women taking antidepressants, including tricyclics and SSRIs (21). Other studies, however, refute this finding.

The effect of antidepressants on gestational age usually finds differences by only a week or less comparing those who have been exposed to antidepressants and those who have not been exposed. Some studies have shown that the effects of SSRIs on gestational age are dependent on the duration of exposure in utero and that longer exposures are more related to preterm birth compared with shorter exposures.

There has been no association between tricyclic use and congenital malformations in pregnancy. The majority of studies also found no link between the rates of heart defects when infants were exposed in the womb. At least one report, however, found a slight link between heart defects and the use of paroxetine (22). These findings have been refuted by other studies.

Babies exposed to an SSRI and a benzodiazepine in the womb may have a higher incidence of congenital heart defects even after controlling depressive symptoms in the mother. Such data indicates that there may be a risk of taking antidepressants along with other types of psychiatric medications.

Other antidepressants such as venlafaxine (Effexor), mirtazapine (Remeron), bupropion (Wellbutrin), and duloxetine (Cymbalta) can be taken in pregnancy. They differ from regular SSRI medications. No studies found an increased risk of congenital defects when compared with people who were either taking other antidepressants or taking medications not known to be teratogenic (23).

The Swedish Medical Birth Registry looked at 732 women who used Serotonin Norepinephrine Reuptake Inhibitor (SNRI) or Norepinephrine Reuptake Inhibitor (NRI) medications in early pregnancy and found that the rate of preterm delivery was significantly increased in those who took those medications, and there was an increase in neonatal symptoms, such as low Apgar scores, respiratory difficulty, newborn seizures, and hypoglycemia. There was no increase in congenital defects or in stillbirth rate (24).

Newborn Behavioral Outcomes

Exposure to tricyclic antidepressants in the womb have been associated with an increase in newborn complications, including seizures, irritability, and jitteriness. Among serotonin reuptake inhibitors, "poor neonatal adaptation" has been found in the first days after exposure to SSRIs during pregnancy. Common symptoms include rapid breathing, newborn hypoglycemia, irritability, temperature instability, seizures, and a weak or absent cry (25). These symptoms were found in 15–30 percent of infants exposed to SSRIs later in the pregnancy. Symptoms in newborns were fortunately short lived and were resolved within two weeks of delivery.

The baby's in the NICU, what did I do wrong? It must be my fault, I think of every cigarette I smoked during the pregnancy, it's my fault. One time I got sick and I took medicine, it's my fault. – New mom

Other Complications

Another complication in newborns exposed to antidepressants in utero includes persistent pulmonary hypertension. This was found to occur in infants exposed late in the pregnancy. Babies with persistent pulmonary hypertension have a right-to-left shunting of blood through the foramen ovale and ductus arteriosus, resulting in hypoxia. Right heart failure can come out of this. The normal rate of this problem is between 0.2 and 2 per 1,000 births and is lethal in about 10 percent of cases. Those exposed to SSRIs in pregnancy have a rate of this of about 3 to 6 in 1,000 babies. Women with longer exposures to SSRIs in pregnancy might be at a higher risk for respiratory difficulties when compared with infants with less exposure (26).

Long-Term Effects on the Baby

There is very limited information on the possible long-term effects of SSRI exposure of an infant in the womb. There were not neurocognitive deficits at six to nine months after the mother used SSRIs in pregnancy in one study (27). The same findings occurred in women taking tricyclic antidepressants.

It is not easily distinguishable whether any cognitive deficits are due to psychotropic exposure during pregnancy or to the effects of the depression itself. There may be developmental delay for children of anxious or depressed parents that are independent of exposure to antidepressant medications. Attention needs to be paid to things like aggression, arousal dysregulation, and attention, which are early indicators of mental disorders.

Electroconvulsive Therapy (ECT) in Pregnancy

ECT has been found to be safe in pregnancy when the depression is extremely severe, such as when the woman has severe suicidality or fails to respond to SSRI therapy. When carefully monitored, there is no evidence that ECT is harmful to both the fetus and the mother (28).

Efficacy of Antidepressants in Pregnancy

There are no studies on the efficacy of antidepressants in pregnant women who are depressed. On the other hand, there is little reason to believe that the response to antidepressants would be any different when compared with nonpregnant women.

It is ideal to evaluate the woman prior to conception, although that is often not possible. About three million pregnancies in the United States are unintended per year. There are algorithms for the management of women who are contemplating to get pregnant but are depressed. They take into account how long a woman has been on the antidepressant and how severe the depression is at the time of conception. Some women are simply too depressed to stop taking an antidepressant and should continue on the medication despite the risk.

Before prescribing any medication to pregnant women, the doctor needs to document all environmental and drug exposures dating from the time of conception to the time the antidepressant was prescribed. The doctor also needs to carefully document that a risk versus benefit discussion has taken place prior to giving the woman her medications (108).

When a depressed woman presents prior to conceiving a baby, the doctor should determine whether or not the patient has moderate or severe symptoms. If the patient has suicidal or psychotic symptoms, she should be referred to psychiatry for aggressive management. This is the type of patient that may wish to wait before becoming pregnant. Antidepressant therapy should be continued until the person is stable. Antidepressants should be taken for at least six to twelve months after being started for an acute episode of depression.

Patients with no symptoms for six months or longer may be able to taper off and stop the antidepressants prior to becoming pregnant. The psychiatrist and obstetrician should coordinate with the patient on how to taper off the medication. A 25 percent reduction in dose every one to two weeks along with close monitoring is usually preferable.

Patients who have a history of severe major depression in the past, bipolar disorder, psychosis, or other psychiatric disease (or who has attempted suicide) may not be candidates for stopping their medication. They should then continue on the antidepressant, with careful monitoring of her obstetrical condition. Psychotherapy may also have to be added to the medication therapy.

It is relatively common to diagnose untreated depression while caring for the pregnant mother or encounter patients who have stopped their medications and are now symptomatic. If the patient is suicidal or psychotic in pregnancy, she should be referred to psychiatry for management. If possible, antiseizure medications should be avoided in the first trimester of pregnancy. These have teratogenic properties and are only appropriate if psychotherapy is ineffective.

The treatment choice for pregnant women should depend on the safety profile of the medications, the state of gestation, the history of the patient's illness, the patient's symptoms, and the therapeutic preferences of the patient and the doctor. An increase in the second half of pregnancy may be necessary because of increased liver metabolism during that time (109).

If the pregnant mother has an agitated depressant, a tricyclic antidepressant can be used as this is more sedating. Mirtazapine (Remeron) is also a sedating medication, but there is little information on its use in pregnancy. Tricyclics and some SSRIs may increase the patient's appetite if she has problems gaining weight. Women who are depressed and who smoke may benefit from taking bupropion, although bulimia and a history of seizures mean you can't use this medication.

If the woman is already taking antidepressants and is pregnant, a consultation with a psychiatrist is necessary if she is currently suicidal or psychotic. If the patient is stable but prefers to take the medication, the psychiatrist and obstetrician should discuss the risks versus benefits of taking the medication in pregnancy. The woman's preference should be documented in her chart. Women who are pregnant and depressed are perhaps in the best position to understand what would happen if she stopped the medication.

Women who have a history of recurrent, severe depression are at a higher risk of relapse if medication is stopped. The risk of relapse is about six times higher in women who stopped their antidepressant in pregnancy compared with those who stopped their antidepressant even if stable at the time.

What if I never get better?

—*Depressed pregnant woman*

If a woman is pregnant and is on antidepressants but is still symptomatic, she may be a good candidate for psychotherapy along with antidepressant use. Women who do not do well on psychotherapy alone should be allowed to continue or restart their antidepressant medication. On the other hand, if the woman is stable and has responded well to psychotherapy in the past, she is a good candidate for monitoring without starting an antidepressant.

Risks of Failing to Treat Depression in Pregnancy

Some pregnant women need pharmacotherapy during pregnancy as there are some risks to being pregnant and being depressed. The most significant risks include intrauterine growth retardation, low birth weight, and prematurity.

The negative effects of untreated depression on childhood depression have been studied. Things like maladaptive social interaction, higher impulsivity, cognitive difficulties, behavioral problems, and emotional issues have been found to occur (110).

Not treating the depressed mother in pregnancy may also be problematic. Most importantly, it puts her at an increased risk of postpartum depression. Things like increased number of hospital admissions and preeclampsia are related to untreated depression in the pregnant woman. She is more likely to engage in high-risk behaviors such as illicit drug use, alcohol abuse, poor nutrition, and smoking in pregnancy. For these reasons, antidepressant use may be indicated. The relapse rate is higher in women who don't take antidepressants yet are at risk for major depression as mentioned above. In one study, 68 percent of women had a major relapse of their depression compared with only 26 percent of women who stayed on their medications. Those who stopped their medications were three times more likely to be hospitalized or have pregnancy-related complications (111).

My sister had a baby, she didn't act this way, what's is wrong with me?—Pregnant woman

Conclusion: Depression during Pregnancy

For some patients, untreated depression can be tragic, leading to suicide of the woman and her fetus in the worst-case scenario. Antidepressants, on the other hand, should always be prescribed carefully in pregnant women. It is clear from examination of all data that women with clinically serious depression should be offered drug therapy even if they choose not to take it.

*My energy was so high when I couldn't sleep, I would run on
the treadmill, hoping I would finally get tired and sleep.*

—*Hypomanic pregnant woman*

Chapter 4

BIPOLAR DISORDER IN PREGNANCY

Women in pregnancy can develop bipolar disorder symptoms or may have bipolar disorder as a predisposition prior to becoming pregnant. During pregnancy, there can be extreme changes in activity level, explosive outbursts, irritability, sleep disturbances, and abnormal behaviors. The woman can suffer either a manic episode or a depressive episode during pregnancy and, in some cases, can have both.

Common manic symptoms in a bipolar disordered woman in pregnancy include the following:

- Prolonged periods of being overly happy or feeling "high"
- Extreme irritability
- Talking very fast
- Moving from one topic to another in conversation
- Racing thoughts
- Extreme distractibility
- Taking on new projects
- Being extremely restless
- Sleeping very little
- Having unrealistic beliefs in one's abilities
- Engaging in high risk behaviors
- Being impulsive
- Signs a woman is suffering from a bipolar depressive episode include the following:
- Feeling sad or hopeless for a long period of time
- Losing interest in activities that were previously enjoyed
- Feeling slow or fatigued

- Having difficulty in concentration
- Having problems with memory
- Being restless or irritable
- Having an alteration in sleeping or eating habits
- Thinking often of death or suicide
- Attempting suicide

Some women can experience milder forms of the disease, having hypomania or dysthymia that doesn't rise to the level of a full-blown attack. Untreated hypomania can lead to mania, and untreated dysthymia can lead to depression and associated suicidality. A mixed mania/depressive state can occur, in which the woman has difficulty sleeping, feels agitated and energized, yet feels hopeless.

Severe bipolar disorder can lead to symptoms of psychosis. The individual can suffer from hallucinations or delusions of grandeur. The psychotic woman with bipolar disorder may feel as if she has a great deal of money, is someone famous, or has unique powers. Psychosis can occur in the depressive state, in which the woman feels as though she has committed a crime or is somehow ruined. The diagnosis of schizophrenia may wrongly be made in a person with severe bipolar disorder and psychosis.

The woman with bipolar disorder is at an increased risk of using illicit drugs or abusing alcohol. There may be relationship problems or poor performance in work or in school. Sometimes, the diagnosis of bipolar disorder is easy to make, and in other situations, it may mimic other psychiatric disorders.

Bipolar disorder usually lasts a lifetime. Episodes of mania and depression typically come back over time. Between episodes, many people with bipolar disorder are free of symptoms, but some people may have lingering symptoms. Between episodes, the woman may have few symptoms or may have some lingering symptoms of the disorder (34).

Chapter 5

Mood Stabilizers In Pregnancy

Mood stabilizers are used to treat bipolar disorder and are designed to prevent relapses into mania. The problem is that most of the drugs used to treat bipolar disorder in pregnancy carry the risk of birth defects.

Lithium is one of the more commonly used mood stabilizers in bipolar disorder. There have been some concerns about using it in pregnancy, however, because of reports of an elevated risk of heart defects when given in the first trimester. These earlier reports have been since supplanted by reports that exposure to lithium in the first trimester is less than previously thought. The current estimate is about one in one thousand pregnancies or about 0.1 percent.

Other mood stabilizers, on the other hand, have been linked to even greater risk of birth defects. For example, the first trimester use of carbamazepine (Tegretol) has been linked to a risk of neural tube defect (1 percent). The worst mood stabilizer and the worst psychiatric medication used in pregnancy is valproic acid (Depakote). Exposure to high doses of this anticonvulsant or the use of the medication with other anticonvulsant medications seems to increase the risk. Because it has a risk of neural tube defect of between 1 percent and 6 percent, it is often used only when no other medications have been shown to be effective. Unfortunately, women who are already on it when they become pregnant have the risk of teratogenicity even when they don't know they are pregnant.

Exposure to most second-generation antipsychotics are considered fairly safe, but avoid clozapine (Clozaril), iloperidone (Fanapt), and ziprasidone (Geodon).

Valproic acid (Depakote) has also been linked to heart defects, genital abnormalities, limb defects, and craniofacial defects. One study (14) linked exposure to valproic acid (Depakote) in utero with a decrease in neurocognitive abilities compared with controls in children up to three years of age. Newer anticonvulsants used in bipolar disorder are much less studied.

Fortunately, lamotrigine (Lamictal) has not been found to be linked to birth defects when used in pregnancy. The manufacturer (GlaxoSmithKline) created the International Lamotrigine Pregnancy Registry that has so far revealed no increase in congenital abnormalities when the drug is taken in utero. Other reports show an incidence of cleft lip/palate of about 0.9 percent.

Some women have turned to the atypical antipsychotic agents rather than the anticonvulsants in the first trimester of pregnancy. So far, no studies have shown an increase in birth defects when taking this drug. However, it may not stabilize the manic symptoms of bipolar disorder as well as other agents.

Bipolar disorder may need to be treated with medications during the pregnancy. The main medical therapies for bipolar disorder in pregnancy (approved by the US FDA) include the following:

- Lithium
- Antiseizure medications such as lamotrigine, valproic acid, and carbamazepine
- Atypical antipsychotic medication including olanzapine, aripiprazole, quetiapine, ziprasidone, and risperidone

Risks of Taking Mood Stabilizers during Pregnancy

The risk of taking these types of medications include but are not limited to the following:

- Congenital malformations
- Neurobehavioral effects in the infant/child
- Obstetrical complications
- Neonatal complications

There are few long-term research studies of women with bipolar disorder who have been exposed during pregnancy to these drugs. Neurobehavioral effects can result from exposure to these medications in the first trimester of pregnancy.

The timing of malformations possible are as follows:

- Neural tube defects can occur in exposures up to thirty-two days after conception.
- Heart abnormalities can occur in exposures between twenty-one and fifty-six days postconception.
- Cleft lip and palate can occur in exposures between forty-two and sixty-three days postconception.

There can also be craniofacial abnormalities if there are exposures during the first trimester. Because more than half of all pregnancies are unplanned, by the time the woman is aware that she is pregnant, the period in which the fetus is susceptible has already happened. This means that the health care provider must always be aware of those medications which cause the least risk of malformations when taken in by women of childbearing age.

Lithium

Lithium is one of the most commonly used drugs in the treatment of bipolar disorder. There exists an International Registry of Lithium Babies in which it has been reported that there is a four hundred times increase in the rate of heart defects (primarily Ebstein's anomaly) in infants exposed to lithium in the womb. Studies have shown that the risk of Ebstein's abnormality in users of lithium is between one and two per one thousand live births, which is twenty to forty times greater than the rate in the normal population.

The use of lithium has been linked to babies weighing greater than average as well as other neonatal complications such as the following:

- Heart problems
- Hypothyroidism
- Diabetes insipidus
- Lethargy
- Decreased muscle tone
- Respiratory problems
- Liver abnormalities

In one study (35), it was found that women on lithium could have the lithium discontinued around the time of delivery, which lessened the neonatal complications, without causing mood swings in the mother. Long-term data are lacking regarding lithium exposure in pregnancy. In another study of sixty children aged five who were exposed to lithium in the first trimester, there were no neurobehavioral changes compared with siblings who were not exposed to the drug.

Carbamazepine (Tegretol)

Carbamazepine, on the other hand, has known teratogenic effects on the fetus. The rate of neural tube defects is about 0.5–1 percent in these infants. It has been found to be more teratogenic when it is used along with other drugs, especially valproic acid. Carbamazepine has also been linked to low-birth-weight infants and a smaller mean head circumference. The use of carbamazepine has been associated with vitamin K deficiency. This could potentially lead to bleeding problems in the newborn as well as abnormalities of the midface.

Because of this potential, it is recommended that the pregnant woman take 20 mg of vitamin K each day during the pregnancy and that 1 mg vitamin K be given intramuscularly to newborns who have been exposed to carbamazepine in utero.

Lamotrigine (Lamictal)

Lamotrigine shows potential as a medication for bipolar disorder during pregnancy partly because it carries the following attributes:

- It is extremely protective against bipolar depression.
- It is generally well tolerated.
- It has shown to be relatively safe in pregnancy.

The rate of major fetal birth defects after exposure in pregnancy is about 2.6 percent. This is in the same range as birth defects seen in populations not exposed to any drugs. Some increase in birth defects have been reported when the maternal daily dose was higher than 200 mg/day (36). Fortunately, there are no known reports of neonatal complications or long-term problems among infants born after exposure to lamotrigine.

Valproate (Depakote)

Valproic acid or sodium valproate is known to cause neural tube defects, craniofacial defects, and heart defects in the developing fetus. It is also known to have negative effects on infant development (37). Exposure to valproate in the first trimester can lead to neural tube defects at a rate of about 5–9 percent. This effect usually occurs when valproate is used at seventeen to thirty days after conception, and the risk is increased if the serum level of valproate is high.

Brief neonatal withdrawal symptoms have been noted as well, including hypoglycemia, liver toxicity, and withdrawal symptoms, which include jitteriness, feeding problems, irritability, and decreased muscle tone. In addition, neurobehavioral changes have been found in the child, including an increased chance of having mental deficiencies and a higher need for special education. Decreased IQs have also been noted of approximately ten IQ points.

Atypical Antipsychotic Medication/
Second-Generation Antipsychotics

Atypical antipsychotic medications have increasingly been used in children, in bipolar disorder, and in the management of depression. Commonly used antipsychotic medication include olanzapine (Zyprexa), aripiprazole (Abilify), risperidone (Risperdal), quetiapine (Seroquel), and ziprasidone (Geodon). Atypical antipsychotic medication crosses the placental barrier; however, there are few studies on the effect of these drugs on the fetus. The largest study so far has failed to identify any birth defects (38).

The rate of maternal complications has been restricted to studies on olanzapine (Zyprexia), which showed maternal weight gain, preeclampsia, gestational diabetes, and insulin resistance. There are no research studies on postnatal effects on the infant and child.

Typical Antipsychotic Agents/First-Generation Antipsychotics

These drugs are still often used in the treatment of mania in pregnancy. Some believe that these medications have a decreased risk of fetal defects compared with mood stabilizers in pregnant women with bipolar disorder. Phenothiazine medications have been known to be used for hyperemesis gravidarum and psychosis in pregnancy, and there is a large amount of data on the effects of these medications on the fetus.

Alternative Medications

There are other medications sometimes used to treat bipolar disorder in pregnancy, including benzodiazepines, antidepressants, and sedative hypnotics. Because they are rarely used alone, data on the possibility of side effects and problems in pregnancy are lacking.

Electroconvulsive Therapy (ECT)

ECT has few side effects when used in pregnant women and may be less harmful than not treating the bipolar disorder or using medications which may have teratogenic effects. There have been a few reports of congenital malformations in babies born to mothers who had ECT during pregnancy, but there has been no pattern that stands out (39).

The biggest problem is a risk of cardiac arrhythmias in the fetus during ECT therapy. This can be minimized by not using atropine, oxygenating the mother well, avoiding hyperventilation, and elevating the maternal right hip. Monitoring the fetal heart during ECT can help detect and correct any fetal cardiac abnormalities.

I don't feel depressed...
I don't cry... I'm not sad...
But I do feel anxious and panicky...
And my heart races at times, and I feel sweaty...
And I have this tightness in my chest...
And I begin to breathe fast...
And I can't sleep at night...
I didn't want to leave my house for weeks...

—*Anxious pregnant woman*

Chapter 6

ANXIETY IN PREGNANCY

Besides depression, pregnant women are at an increased risk of anxiety during pregnancy. This type of antenatal mood disorder has been shown to have long-lasting effects on the infant, particularly on its psychosocial development. Tests have been done on animal models and are being done in humans.

Being anxious and stressed out during pregnancy is considered to be a normal phenomenon. Some symptoms of anxiety mimic normal symptoms of pregnancy, which make the diagnosis of anxiety in pregnancy very difficult. When women feel anxious all the time and meet the criteria for having generalized anxiety disorder or when they suffer from frequent panic attacks, this is when it can lead to problems in the pregnancy. Some women suffer from a disorder known as "tokophobia" in which they have a specific fear of giving birth.

Common symptoms of anxiety in a pregnancy include the following:

- Constant worry about the pregnancy or the baby's health
- Feeling overly anxious with an inability to control the anxiety
- Feeling irritable
- Having tense muscles
- Having poor sleeping behaviors
- Being unable to concentrate on activities of daily living
- Tiredness
- Feelings of restlessness

If the anxiety escalates to the point in which the woman is suffering from a panic attack, they suffer the symptoms as noted above along with the following symptoms:

- Feeling as if the woman was going crazy
- Feeling an inability to breathe during an attack
- Feeling as though something ominous is about to happen
- Feeling as though the woman might die during the attack
- Having a persistent fear of having another panic attack

Women also have an increased risk of obsessive compulsive disorder during pregnancy. Symptoms of this disorder include the following:

- The presence of recurring, intrusive, and persistent thoughts that cannot be controlled
- Having compulsions designed to relieve the thoughts through repetitive behaviors or recurrent and repetitive thoughts

Panic attacks are often related to the development of physical symptoms so that the woman feels as though she is having a heart attack or has some other type of nonpsychological, physical illness. Depression can go along with the symptoms of anxiety.

Anxiety is extremely common. It is estimated that one out of every ten pregnant women will suffer from some form of anxiety during the pregnancy. People with a preexisting anxiety condition are at a higher risk of developing anxiety during the pregnancy (29).

Common Risk Factors of Anxiety during Pregnancy

There are some risk factors that predispose a woman to having anxiety during pregnancy. These include the following:

- Having a history of panic attacks or anxiety when not pregnant
- Having a strong family history of anxiety and panic attacks
- Using illicit drugs
- Having a history of posttraumatic stress disorder
- Having excess stress during the pregnancy
- Having a history of depression.
- Having a history of premenstrual dysphoric disorder or PMDD
- Being under the age of twenty during the pregnancy
- Having little social support
- Living alone
- Having marital discord
- Being separated, widowed, or divorced

- Having lived through a stressful event within the year prior to the pregnancy
- Having a low income
- Having more than three living children
- Having pregnancy complications
- Being ambivalent about the pregnancy

Certainly, a woman can suffer from anxiety in pregnancy and not have any preexisting anxiety symptoms.

Risks of Not Treating the Anxiety during Pregnancy

There are risks involved in taking medications for anxiety in pregnancy, but there are also clear risks of not treating the anxiety. Some of these include the following:

- The infant having low birth weight
- Suffering from premature birth as defined as delivering before thirty-seven weeks' gestation
- Infant respiratory depression
- Low APGAR scores after delivery
- Increased jitteriness in the infant
- The mother also carries some risks in having the anxiety untreated. These include the following:
- Termination of the pregnancy
- Postpartum anxiety
- Suicide (if depression is also involved)
- Illicit drug use
- Poor attachment to the infant
- Poor personal cares
- Pre-eclampsia
- Cesarean birth
- Preterm labor

Studies in Animals

Animal studies have linked antenatal stress and abnormal behavioral and emotional states in the young. The effects appear to last through adulthood (18). The types of disturbances seen in the animal offspring are far-reaching and include emotional reactivity, behavioral disturbances, cognitive delay, and changes in sexual behavior and neurological development.

In some cases, there have been disturbances in the hypothalamic pituitary adrenal axis (HPA). The effect can be simulated by injecting ACTH (adrenocorticotrophic hormone) into the pregnant animal subject (19). According to research, the young born to mothers who have suffered from some type of antenatal stress end up being overreactive to stressors and secrete more cortisol in response to stress compared with those not under stress. In rodents, this effect has been found to persist through adulthood. In primates, it has been found to last for several years after birth. This means that the HPA axis may be able to be programmed while the offspring is still a fetus.

Serotonergic and dopaminergic systems are also believed to play some sort of role in the development of postnatal problems in those who suffered stress during the prenatal period. The effects of antenatal stress appear to be sensitive to the gestational age of the fetus.

When adoption studies are undertaken, research has shown that having a less stressful postnatal environment can moderate these effects. It means that later interventions can have a positive effect on those who were exposed to stress and anxiety in the prenatal period. Clearly, further studies need to be undertaken to see whether the intervention needs to be early in the postnatal state or whether it can be done later in life.

There are also underlying studies that look into the various genetic factors that play into antenatal anxiety. The genetic effects of the stress response and anxiety are now becoming more understood so that it is possible that there can be a differentiation between genetic and environmental risk factors in the overall postnatal outcome.

Studies in Humans

Most of the research on anxiety in pregnancy in humans have been focused on the outcome of the pregnancy (20). In one study, it was revealed that women who suffered some kind of serious life event during the first trimester of pregnancy showed a 50 percent increase in the chances of having a congenital abnormality in the neural crest or cranial organs. The unexpected death of a child was considered the most severe type of stress, and the risk of malformations in this situation was even greater. Other things, such as preterm labor and a small-for-gestational-age infant, have been closely linked to anxiety in human subjects (21).

In one study, 8,719 women were examined and were given self-reported stress surveys at thirty weeks' gestation. The relative risk for preterm delivery (prior to thirty-seven weeks' gestation) was 1.22 for women under moderate stress and 1.75 for women under high-stress situations in pregnancy. The effect of stress in the first trimester on the obstetrical outcome was not found to be as significant.

In another study (22), women who suffered a severe anxiety-provoking stress in pregnancy had a 50 percent increase in significant prematurity (infants born at less than thirty-four weeks' gestation).

Early studies among humans have been similar to animal studies, revealing a connection between stress and anxiety during pregnancy and emotional or behavioral disturbances in the baby. Some of these studies, however, have been flawed in that they did not take into account other risks for prematurity, such as smoking, and didn't distinguish between stress in the antenatal period and stress in the postnatal period.

A large community study has been undertaken called the Avalon Longitudinal Study of Parents and Children (23). In this study, maternal anxiety in the third trimester of pregnancy was found to be linked to the development of behavior and emotional issues in children when they reached the age of four years. The link held up after it was controlled for anxiety in the mother on four different postnatal periods up to the age of thirty-three months. After the researchers had controlled the study for obstetric, antenatal, and socioeconomic risk factors, many indicators of postnatal anxiety, and both antenatal and postnatal depression, it was found that when women reported anxiety at thirty-two weeks into the pregnancy, there were significant behavioral and emotional issues in the development of both girls and boys. In particular, inattention and hyperactivity in boys was found to be significantly linked to anxiety in the latter part of the pregnancy.

The same study also showed a significant link between anxiety in pregnancy and the infant/child's neurological development. When there was elevated anxiety in the mother at eighteen weeks into the pregnancy, things like mixed handedness in the child were noted at four years of age. This was found to be independent of the handedness of both the mother and the father as well as other antenatal risk factors. There was no similar association found in postnatal anxiety, showing that anxiety in the mother was qualitatively different in the effects it had during or after the pregnancy.

If mixed handedness is truly related to anxiety during pregnancy, this could mean that other conditions associated with mixed handedness like autism and dyslexia could also be related to antenatal anxiety.

There have been several different mechanisms connecting antenatal anxiety and disturbances in the child that have been put forth. Antenatal anxiety may cause problems in the infant because it shortens the time before birth and reduces birth rate. Premature birth is perhaps the greatest perinatal risk factor for things like ADHD and schizophrenia in the child. Being small for gestational age is also related to emotional and behavioral problems (24).

There is increasing evidence relating to the HPA axis and anxiety during pregnancy. In one study (25), it was revealed that both the fetal and maternal levels of cortisol were correlated. This means that at least some maternal cortisol is able to cross the placenta and can significantly change fetal exposure. Other studies have shown that increased levels of anxiety in the mother during the later stages of pregnancy (but not early in pregnancy) caused a reduction in blood flow and an increased resistance index in the uterine arteries leading to the fetus. High resistance has been found to be linked to poor obstetrical outcome, including preeclampsia and intrauterine growth retardation. This may be the explanation as to why mothers who are anxious have infants that are born with low birth weights for their gestational age.

The fetus reacts differently to the mother's mood in pregnancy at different stages of the pregnancy because the fetus has different vulnerabilities that vary with the stage of the fetus's development. This means that severe anxiety in early pregnancy, when most of the major organs are being developed, can affect the physical features of the infant and can lead to things such as cleft palate. If the anxiety occurs further on in the pregnancy, the brain is the major organ being developed, and this can have a greater effect on emotional and behavioral measures.

The Risk of Preeclampsia in Untreated Anxiety during Pregnancy

A study was undertaken to evaluate the risk of preeclampsia in women who were not treated for anxiety during pregnancy (26). The study was performed in Helsinki with both depression and anxiety in pregnancy evaluated. Preeclampsia was defined as having a blood pressure of greater than 140/90 and proteinuria.

A total of six hundred twenty one first-time pregnancies were evaluated at between ten and seventeen weeks' gestation and at the time of delivery. A total of 4.5 percent of women developed preeclampsia during the study. Depression had an odds ratio of 2.5, and anxiety had an odds ratio of 3.2 for the development of preeclampsia. Interestingly, the risk was even greater if the woman also suffered from bacterial vaginosis during the pregnancy.

Effect of Anxiety on Assisted Reproduction

A study was undertaken that looked into the role of anxiety on the outcome among women treated for reproductive difficulties (26). In the study, 281 women took part in a study on depression and anxiety and IVF outcome. The women filled out the State and Trait Anxiety Inventory in order to measure their level of anxiety and the Beck Depression Inventory in order to measure their level of depression. It was found that there was a strong relationship between the psychological state of the woman and her probability of becoming pregnant following an IVF procedure.

In the study, it was found that being anxious prior to IVF procedures had a greater impact on the ability to get pregnant using an IVF procedure than did depression. It was determined on the basis of these findings that psychological counseling may be in order for women contemplating an IVF procedure.

Women who are undergoing IVF therapy are often already anxious and/ or depressed because they cannot get pregnant through normal means. They may be concerned about the treatment being given to them as a result of their infertility (27). In fact, there are data suggesting that there is a strong relationship between the psychological state of the mother and the state of being infertile. Other studies support the idea that a woman's distress level during the time of assisted reproductive therapies plays a role in the success of the treatments (28).

One study took place in the Netherlands. Women who underwent IVF treatments between January 1999 and March 2000 took part in the research. Only the first treatment cycle was used in the study. A maximum of two embryos were transferred into the women's uteruses. The women were asked to take part in surveys on their psychological state. A total of 291 women participated in the study. The women took the State and Trait Anxiety Inventory to measure their level of anxiety. Depression was measured by the Beck Depression Inventory.

The researchers measured the number of follicles each woman had, the number of embryos that were created, and the pregnancy status of the women. The study participants had different reasons for their infertility including female factor infertility, male factor infertility, and combined factor infertility. The results showed a negative relationship between anxiety and achieving a pregnancy. The combination of anxiety and depression was even more so related to the ability to become pregnant.

Chapter 7

TREATMENT OF ANXIETY
IN PREGNANCY

Women in pregnancy who are anxious may be treated with medical or nonmedical treatments. Cognitive behavioral therapy has been proposed as a general psychotherapeutic technique to help women who suffer from anxiety during pregnancy (31).

Using cognitive behavioral therapeutic techniques, the woman can learn the following tools to reduce anxiety:

- Learning how to say "no" to things that increase the level of distress and anxiety
- Cutting back on chores and increasing relaxation time
- Taking time off from work
- Practicing yoga, deep breathing exercises, or stretching
- Increasing exercise and doing things like walking or swimming
- Eating a well-balanced diet.
- Increasing the time spent sleeping.
- Joining a therapy or support group related to anxiety and pregnancy
- Taking omega-3 fatty acid supplements, which have been found to improve psychological symptoms

Antianxiety medications will be discussed later but can be used to control severe anxiety disorders during pregnancy.

Medications for Anxiety in Pregnancy

There is controversy over whether or not a woman should take benzodiazepines during pregnancy. Several studies have shown no increase in risk of birth defects after pregnant women took benzodiazepines in the first trimester of pregnancy. In particular, recent reports have revealed no increase in cleft lip/palate in those who took benzodiazepines. If the risk exists, it is about 0.7 percent, which is a tenfold increase in cleft lip/palate compared with people in the normal population. Overall, the risk of taking benzodiazepines in the first trimester is less than one percent among all congenital abnormalities.

There is limited data on the safety of medications for anxiety that are not benzodiazepines such as buspirone (Buspar) or hypnotic medications like zaleplon (Sonata) and zolpidem (Ambien) often used for sleep. For this reason, the use of these medications in pregnancy should be extremely limited or not used at all. Zolpidem (Ambien) has not been shown to affect conception, so it can be used during infertility treatment.

Pregnancy is a time of great excitement and emotional changes for couples. Unfortunately, for some, it has been associated with increased stress and anxiety. The levels of gonadal steroids have been found in pregnancy with elevations of estrogen as high as one hundred times nonpregnant levels and elevations in progesterone as high as one thousand times nonpregnant levels. These changes can cause an increase in emotional difficulties (112).

There may be psychological factors in play when a woman develops anxiety during pregnancy. The mother can develop concerns over the health of her fetus, and there may be a change in the woman's lifestyle after the child's birth, worry over finances, and worry about being a good mother that can cause anxiety in pregnancy. The pregnancy may be unwanted or unexpected, which furthers symptoms of anxiety and stress. Some women will also become aware of painful past life events regarding their own parents.

While pregnancy alone can bring on anxiety, there are some women who have preexisting anxiety disorders during pregnancy. Most studies have looked into the effects on pregnancy among women with preexisting panic disorder and obsessive compulsive disorder rather than on those with generalized anxiety disorder.

Although childbirth may lead to developing panic disorder for the first time, the effects of pregnancy on preexisting panic disorder have been mixed. In one study (113) of forty-nine women with panic disorder, about 20 percent were found to improve during pregnancy, while 20 percent worsened, and 54 percent remained the same.

Women with milder panic disorder may improve during pregnancy; however, women with more severe symptoms may have a worsening of their panic disorder during pregnancy. Pregnancy is not protective against anxiety and panic disorder, and the postpartum period may make the woman even more vulnerable to a worsening of symptoms. Anxiety disorders themselves may affect the pregnancy outcomes.

In one review, panic disorder and generalized anxiety disorder were studied along with the impact of untreated anxiety disorder on pregnancy and potential adverse reactions of taking medications for anxiety during pregnancy (114).

Panic Disorder

This disorder is different from the sudden and persistent fear that can be brought about by exposure to or anticipation of a specific situation or object. It is more common in women with an onset of about the midtwenties. This coincides with peak childbearing years. The prevalence of panic disorder in adults is about 5 percent, although the exact prevalence in pregnancy is not known.

Among the most common conditions associated with panic disorder is depression, with up to two-thirds of patients who have panic disorder also having an episode of major depression at some point in their life. This can complicate things and can lead to an increased risk of suicide when both conditions exist at once. Other comorbid conditions include social anxiety disorder.

Generalized Anxiety Disorder

Anxiety disorders are extremely common, with about 30 percent of women suffering from an anxiety disorder at some point in their lives (115). A total of 65 percent of patients with generalized anxiety disorder have other mental disorders such as panic disorder, depression, and agoraphobia. Generalized anxiety disorder tends to be a severely disabling condition with a chance of having a comorbid disorder as high as 90 percent.

The goals of treatment for generalized anxiety disorder include treatment of the worry, tension, autonomic arousal, and somatic distress. The evaluation for anxiety disorders in pregnancy should involve complete examination, including liver function tests, kidney tests, thyroid testing, and a complete blood count, especially if treatment seems to be ineffective. A urine toxicology screen should be done because of the high incidence of drug use among anxious pregnant women. Herbal medications and over-the-counter medications should be evaluated as some can make anxiety disorders worse.

About 91 percent of patients with panic disorder and 84 percent of those with agoraphobia have at least one other psychiatric condition (115). At least half of all panic disorder patients also have depression. About one-third of people with both disorders have depression which precedes the panic disorder. About two-thirds have their first panic attack during or after a diagnosis of depression.

Other comorbidities include social phobia, a specific phobia, posttraumatic stress disorder, and generalized anxiety disorder. Less common comorbidities include personality disorders, hypochondriasis, and substance abuse issues.

Failing to Treat Anxiety in Pregnancy

There is little research on the long-term risk to the fetus exposed to untreated psychiatric disorders in utero. Overall, it has been suggested that not treating anxiety in pregnancy can lead to lower gestational age at the time of birth, low birth weight, impairment of fetal movement, low Apgar scores, and impairment of fetal hemodynamics (114).

One study linked anxiety in early pregnancy with the development of preeclampsia by a factor of threefold (116). There was a reported link between anxiety and cervical dyskinesia, cesarean section risk, and premature rupture of membranes. Panic attacks during pregnancy can also lead to poor nutrition, the use of harmful medications or drugs as a way to self-treat the disorder, fetal distress, and placental abruption. Agoraphobia, along with panic disorder, also impairs getting adequate prenatal care, which can affect the pregnancy outcome.

Medication Use during Pregnancy

Pregnancy affects the absorption, distribution, metabolism, and elimination of drugs used to treat anxiety. There are decreases in gastric emptying and intestinal motility that increase the absorption of medications in the small intestines (117). The woman's plasma volume and amount of extracellular fluid volume increase dramatically. In addition, there is an increase in body fat in pregnancy which increases the volume of distribution of lipophilic psychotropic drugs. Pregnancy is also associated with numerous changes in metabolism by the liver. In addition, drug elimination during pregnancy is affected by an increase in blood flow through the kidneys as well as the glomerular filtration rate (117).

Because psychotropic drugs cross the placental barrier, they may have an important impact on the development of the fetus. For this reason, it is necessary to balance the effects of medication use with the chances of fetal compromise if the disorder is left untreated.

Antidepressants such as SSRIs and SNRIs have been used during pregnancy for the management of anxiety despite a lack of strong data suggesting they are safe. Drugs for anxiety and depression should be used when the benefits far outweigh the risks of fetal exposure to these drugs. The issue of psychotropic drugs in pregnancy is not yet resolved although animal studies on SSRIs in pregnancy have shown no teratogenicity (118).

In the mother, drugs such as citalopram (Celexa), fluvoxamine (Luvox), and sertraline (Zoloft) have the highest incidence of gastrointestinal effects, including nausea, vomiting, and diarrhea. Nausea and diarrhea are usually dose dependent and are transient. Most patients initially lose weight, although up to one-third will gain weight. Headaches happen in about 20 percent of these women, and some will develop difficulty sleeping or too much sleeping. Fluoxetine (Prozac) is the most likely to cause insomnia, which is often taken in the morning to counteract that side effect.

Paroxetine (Paxil) and citalopram (Celexa) are most likely to cause fatigue rather than insomnia. Extrapyramidal symptoms can be seen in fluoxetine when given in doses greater than 40 mg per day. In rare circumstances, SSRIs are related to hyponatremia and platelet dysfunction. Venlafaxine has been found to be better tolerated than some, although side effects of dry mouth, somnolence, nausea, nervousness, constipation, anorexia, blurry vision, anxiety, and weakness have been found to occur.

Abruptly stopping most SSRIs except fluoxetine may produce a discontinuation syndrome, which results in somnolence, insomnia, or nausea. Antidepressants should be gradually tapered over two to four weeks (except fluoxetine, which can just be stopped). Those taking venlafaxine in doses higher than 300 mg per day have been found to suffer from high blood pressure when the drug is stopped abruptly (119).

There are several things to be concerned about when using antianxiety medications in pregnancy and in the postpartum state. This includes perinatal syndromes, infant neurobehavioral issues, and teratogenicity. All antianxiety medications pass through the placental barrier and have implications regarding the development of the fetus.

Teratogenicity is especially problematic in the first trimester and occurs when the drug causes birth defects greater than the current rate of birth defects as a baseline, which is 2 percent. To date, there have been no significant effects to the fetus of giving SSRIs to pregnant women. Most of the data available have been on the use of fluoxetine. There is a register of more than two thousand cases of patients treated with fluoxetine that have shown no increase in birth defects from prenatal exposure to the drug. Citalopram (Celexa) has also been studied without findings of teratogenicity (120). Studies on venlafaxine and mirtazapine have also been found to be safe.

On the other hand, the risk of using benzodiazepines in pregnancy is less clear. In one study (120), there was a risk of cleft lip and palate associated with benzodiazepine use. The risk was small at less than 1 percent compared with 0.06 percent in normal individuals.

Perinatal syndromes have been associated with the use of anxiolytic therapy. Very small studies have been done indicating withdrawal symptoms in babies exposed to SSRIs in the third trimester (121). Common symptoms included irritability, tremulousness, jitteriness, myoclonus, difficulty sleeping, and difficulty feeding. Two infants exposed to paroxetine (Paxil) developed necrotizing enterocolitis. Infants may be more sensitive to paroxetine withdrawal because of its short half-life. Fluoxetine exposure, on the other hand, was unassociated with withdrawal symptoms with the exception of having a higher incidence of admissions to the special care nursery.

Tricyclic antidepressants are also effective against anxiety; however, exposure to these drugs in the third trimester has been found to be more problematic. There have been case reports of problems with irritability, perinatal adaptation, seizures, and jitteriness when the mother used tricyclics in the third trimester. Cases of bowel obstruction and urinary retention have also been reported (121).

Data on using benzodiazepines in the third trimester have shown significant risk to the infant. The most common side effects include infant sedation and withdrawal symptoms. This includes low Apgar scores, muscular weakness, sluggish response to cold temperature, and hypothermia in the infant (122). Symptoms that occur are believed to be due to benzodiazepine withdrawal, including excessive crying, hyperreflexia, hypertonia, bradycardia, tremors, restlessness, seizures, irritability, cyanosis, and abnormal sleep patterns.

These types of effects have been noted for several months following the birth and vary according to the amount of exposure and length of exposure in utero. Clearly, the effects of benzodiazepine withdrawal have been found to be more serious than those resulting from SSRI withdrawal (123).

There may be neurobehavioral effects over the long term in children exposed to psychotropic medications in utero. Data on fluoxetine (Prozac), however, have shown no neurobehavioral effects.

When it comes to benzodiazepine exposure, the data are mixed. One study (124) showed deviant motor development at six and ten months in children exposed to benzodiazepines in utero. These same children at eighteen months tested at nearly normal levels after benzodiazepine exposure. Other studies have shown delays in social abilities, hearing, and speech variables among children exposed to benzodiazepines.

Benzodiazepines Used in Pregnancy

Besides SSRIs, benzodiazepines have been used to treat anxiety in pregnancy. They vary primarily in their half-life and length of effectiveness. Some benzodiazepines used in pregnancy include the following:

- Alprazolam (Xanax)
- Clonazepam (Klonopin)

- Clorazepate (Tranzene)
- Chlordiazepoxide (Librium)
- Valium (diazepam)
- Ativan (lorazepam)
- Oxazepam (Serax)
- Temazepam (Restoril)
- Triazolam (Halcion)

Conclusion of Treatment of Anxiety in Pregnancy

When faced with the decision to use a psychotropic medication for anxiety in pregnancy, the goal is to maximize the effectiveness of the medication so that the fetus is not associated with side effects related to having the mental illness. The most important thing to consider is whether or not the patient has had a positive response to a given medication in the past. A new medication should not be started while the woman is pregnant or nursing.

Since it is impossible to have a complete list of all the risks of taking a psychotropic drug, it is important to discuss with the patient the risk of taking the medication versus the risk of not treating the illness. This conversation should be clearly documented in the patient's medical record.

They should know the following:

- Nonpharmacological therapy is always available as an alternative to medication.
- Benzodiazepines can cause side effects and withdrawal symptoms in the newborn.
- The lowest effective dose will be used to treat the anxiety.
- Keeping the dose low around the time of delivery may eliminate infant withdrawal symptoms.
- SSRIs are the first line of therapy as they have the least potential for fetal and infant problems.
- Abruptly stopping medications for panic disorder is not recommended due to the high risk of withdrawal and relapse.
- Women who are not taking the medications during pregnancy should consider starting them again after delivery because there is a high risk of relapse in the postpartum state.

When I lay down, I feel anxious, I can't go to sleep. The list
of things I need to do goes round and round in my head. I
worry I'm not a good enough mother. I just can't relax.

—Anxious pregnant woman

I began to believe that I was a bad mom.
And that I should never have had children...
Why would I think such horrible things
over and over again...
When will these thoughts stop?

Obsessive Compulsive Disorder in Pregnancy

Both pregnant and postpartum women are believed to be at a higher risk of obsessive compulsive disorder (OCD) compared with the general population. When the problem is diagnosed in postpartum women, it can negatively impact the maternal-infant relationship and infant development. One research study (32) looked into the risk of developing OCD while pregnant. They evaluated twelve primary research studies involving OCD and pregnancy as well as seven studies on OCD in the postpartum state. The women were evaluated using structured diagnostic interviews, and each study had age and regionally matched controls.

It was discovered that there was indeed an increased risk of OCD in pregnancy and during the postpartum period. Women in pregnancy had an average risk of OCD of 2.07 percent compared with a risk of 1.08 percent in the normal population. Postpartum women suffered from OCD at a rate of 2.43 percent. This resulted in a near doubling of the risk of obsessive compulsive disorder among pregnant women and an even higher risk in postpartum women.

The exact cause of OCD is considered unknown. There is one theory that says it is related to serotonin levels in the brain, but in fact, certain antidepressants that raise serotonin levels can calm OCD symptoms. In pregnancy, fluctuations of estrogen and progesterone may cause dysfunction of the serotonergic system, leading to obsessive compulsive disorder. There is another theory that the rapid increase in oxytocin at the end of pregnancy and during the immediate postpartum state might trigger the onset of OCD.

Clinical Findings of OCD in Pregnancy

Many of these women develop obsessions that are directly related to the pregnancy or the neonate. They develop fears of contaminating their baby and have concerns about doing things in an exact, specific way. They fear intentionally or accidentally hurting the baby and have behaviors linked to excessive cleaning, washing the baby, checking on the baby, and avoidance compulsions.

I'm worried the hospital gave me the wrong baby. I'm afraid to love this baby because someone will come and get her because they made a mistake. How I know she's mine? I try to pretend she is there is always the question inside my mind. What if she someone else's baby. —Woman with OCD

A woman who develops OCD in the perinatal period can have interference with the maternal-infant bond. She can avoid the infant altogether or become excessively involved in the infant's care. It has been suggested that these behaviors can affect the cognitive-behavioral development in the infant. The mother's obsessions and compulsions can also affect her interactions with other family members as well.

I'm worried the babies going to choke, I put all my other kids on soft foods, because what if I can't get to them while I'm feeding the baby?

—Mom with OCD

There are no documented instances of a woman with pure OCD intentionally harming the baby, but women with OCD and other psychiatric diagnoses, including psychosis, can harm their infant. Untreated OCD can have longstanding effects on both the mothers and their infants.

I thought of putting my thumb through that soft spot on his head (the fontanelle). I knew it was illogical, but I still thought about doing it. I didn't do it.

—Mom with OCD-type symptoms

Mothers with OCD often say that they can't enjoy their babies, and the children have been seen to suffer from a wide range of internalizing disorders, including having OCD themselves.

I do not feel loving toward my baby and can't even go through the motions to take care of him/her.

—Mom with OCD and depression

49

The most common coexisting disorders with OCD in pregnancy is major depression. The same is true in postpartum women. Women with OCD during pregnancy run a higher risk of postpartum depressive symptoms occurring about two to three weeks after the onset of the symptoms of OCD.

Women who have OCD symptoms during or shortly after pregnancy may not recognize that their symptoms are part of some type of mental illness and may not attempt to seek help. Predictors of OCD in and around pregnancy include having a family history of OCD and having a history of premenstrual dysphoric disorder.

OCD should be screened by family practitioners and obstetricians, especially in women with a history of the disorder prior to pregnancy. Screening can be done by directly asking about obsessive thoughts and compulsive behaviors related to the pregnancy or to the care of the infant. This should be done throughout the pregnancy and in the first few weeks after the baby is delivered. Those who are screened positively for OCD should be referred to psychiatry for evaluation of other psychiatric disorders, particularly depression.

I'd lock myself in my room because I thought of throwing the baby against the wall when he cries. —Depressed mom with OCD symptoms

The treatment of obsessive compulsive disorder is extremely challenging. Only about 20 percent of patients who are not pregnant and who have OCD actually go into a complete remission. Treating OCD in pregnancy and in breast-feeding moms is even more difficult because the obsessions are usually related to infant and fetal safety. The patient may refuse to take any kind of psychotropic medication to control the disease out of fear of harming the fetus.

The first line of treatment for OCD in pregnancy is cognitive behavioral therapy. The use of selective serotonin reuptake inhibitors has also been used to manage the disorder in pregnancy, especially if there is also depression present. If these types of drugs are used near term, the infant should be watched in the first forty-eight hours of life for jitteriness, poor feeding, and breathing difficulties as they withdraw from the medication.

All SSRIs, except fluoxetine (Prozac), are found in extremely low levels in breast milk and are not expected to cause any problems in breastfed babies. Fluoxetine (Prozac) has slightly higher levels of the drug in breastfed infants, and things like drowsiness, poor weight gain, and colic have been reported in breastfed babies exposed to fluoxetine (Prozac).

Because recurrences with subsequent pregnancies is likely, it is not out of the question to prophylactically treat a woman who has had a history of postpartum

OCD in previous pregnancies. The treatment should be maintained for at least one year after the delivery of the baby as long as there has been some therapeutic response. If the medication is stopped too soon, relapses are likely. If medications are considered in pregnancy, it should be done on a case-by-case basis with the risks weighed against the benefits (33).

I heard voices while I was in the shower telling me
I should go ahead and just kill myself.

—Andrea Yates

Chapter 8

PSYCHOSIS IN PREGNANCY

Women in pregnancy can have a preexisting psychosis or can develop psychosis in pregnancy. There is a limited amount of data on the course of schizophrenia in pregnancy. Some women appear to have an improvement in their symptom, while others will have a worsening of their symptoms.

Regardless of how the psychosis is going, women who have had psychosis in the past need close monitoring by their primary health care provider and their psychiatrist during the pregnancy. Psychosis can be devastating to the mother and fetus as often, women fail to get adequate prenatal care during pregnancy. It also lead to suicide in the mother, infanticide, prematurity, and low birth weights in the neonate. It is vital to treat acute psychosis in pregnancy, which can involve increasing social support, drug therapy, electroconvulsive therapy, and hospitalization if necessary (40).

Women who suffer from psychotic disorders during pregnancy carry a greater chance of having psychiatric and obstetric complications. Recent research has shown decreased fertility rate in women who have schizophrenia. Relapse of psychosis in pregnancy is uncommon, but women who have affective psychosis (psychosis as part of a mood disorder) carry a higher risk of relapse after delivery.

There is a higher risk of obstetrical complications, including the possibility of stillbirth and deaths in the neonatal period. There is also a possible link to sudden infant death syndrome and psychosis in pregnancy. One study revealed that there is a 27 percent risk of having a psychotic episode and a 38 percent risk of a nonpsychotic episode in the first twelve months after birth.

Women with nonaffective psychosis have a higher risk of developing postpartum depression compared with control subjects. The consequences of not treating psychosis in pregnancy can be significant and, after the birth, can lead to infanticide. Suicide during the pregnancy is also possible. Because of this, doctors need to help the woman weigh the risk of exposure to the drugs by the fetus against the risk of not treating the psychosis (41).

Symptoms of Psychosis

Women who develop a psychotic disorder in pregnancy have their own set of symptoms related to their individual circumstances. There are four main symptoms you can find in any psychotic disorder, including delusions, hallucinations, lack of insight and awareness, and confused or disturbed thoughts.

- Hallucinations. This is the experience of seeing or hearing something that doesn't really exist. In actuality, hallucinations can involve all five senses including some of the following symptoms:
- Visual hallucinations. Seeing shapes, colors, people, or animals that aren't really there.
- Auditory hallucinations. The woman may hear voices, some of which may be angry, sarcastic, or otherwise unpleasant. Often, they hear a mumble of pejorative voices. Some have ongoing conversations and command hallucinations telling them to harm themselves.
- Tactile hallucinations. The woman may feel as though she is being touched when no one is actually there.
- Olfactory hallucinations. The woman may experience an unpleasant or unusual smell.
- Gustatory hallucinations. The woman may experience an unpleasant taste in the mouth that doesn't go away.
- Delusions. When the woman has delusions, she has a continual belief that something others see as bizarre or implausible is true. Two examples of delusions are paranoid delusions and delusions of grandeur. People who suffer from psychosis often feel as though someone or an organization is planning to harm or kill them. This results in abnormal behavior. The woman may refuse to be associated with cell phones because she believes that they are listening devices that are keeping track of her. She may believe she is someone famous or that she has a special power that no one else has.
- Confused or disturbed thinking. The woman will have confused thinking and disrupted patterns of thought. Evidence of this can be seen in the following:
  - Random speech in which she switches the topic of discussion, often in the middle of a sentence.
  - Rapid or continual speech

o   Sudden loss in her train of thought, which results in pauses in activity or conversation

My doctor told me to take a warm bath to relax, but I'm afraid it will boil the baby, so I didn't.

- Lack of insight. These women are often completely unaware that their behavior is strange or that the hallucinations and delusions are not actually real. They may be able to see this type of behavior in others but cannot see it in themselves. They may complain about the mental unwellness of their roommate in a psychiatric hospital but may not see the same behavior in themselves as being abnormal (42).

The Outcome of Infants in Women with Psychosis

There is little research done on the outcomes of pregnancies among women who suffer from a psychotic disorder while pregnant. One study has looked into this and has studied the antenatal care of women who had a history of psychosis as well as the obstetrical outcomes and the health of the babies after birth.

The study looked at women who gave birth between 1996 and 1998. Some of them were psychotic, and others were not. The psychotic population amounted to 199 cases with a nonpsychotic control population of 787 women.

Research has shown that women with schizophrenia begin receiving prenatal care much later than the control group (43). They are also more likely to have problems with the birth, such as fetal and neonatal demise. There has also been very little research looking into the subsequent health of infants born to women with psychosis.

The hypotheses of the study included the following:

- That women with psychosis receive prenatal care at a later date in their pregnancy than women without psychosis.
- That women with psychosis have a greater chance of obstetrical complications and perinatal deaths compared with those without psychosis.
- That there is a higher rate of neonatal and infant deaths in children of mothers suffering from psychosis.
- That the infants of psychotic mothers have a greater likelihood of nonaccidental and accidental injuries.
- That infants of psychotic mothers have more hospital referrals and more visits to the emergency room compared with controls.

The study made use of the General Practice Research Database (44), which combines information from as many as 480 medical practices in England between 1996 and 1999. There were 199 psychotic mothers used in the study aged seventeen to forty-two years. Each psychotic mother was matched with up to four control cases.

The women who had a psychotic disorder had the following psychiatric diagnoses: schizophrenia, paranoid psychosis, psychosis not otherwise specified, manic depressive psychosis, depressive psychosis, puerperal psychosis, schizoaffective psychosis, and drug-induced psychosis. Nineteen percent of women who were classified as controls were identified as having some kind of psychiatric history that was not related to psychosis.

Eight percent of cases were admitted for psychiatric reasons sometime during their pregnancy. Four percent of the psychotic women took an overdose during the pregnancy, while no member of the control group suffered an overdose or had a psychiatric admission during the pregnancy.

A total of 20 percent of psychotic women needed a cesarean section compared with 14 percent among the control group. Those with psychosis were less likely to receive contraceptive advice after the delivery of their infant compared with controls. There was a significantly greater number of stillbirths among psychotic women compared with controls. None of those in the control group had a neonatal death compared with 2 percent in the psychosis group. There was only one case of SIDS (sudden infant death syndrome) among the psychotic mothers and no cases of SIDs in the control group.

Fortunately, there were no differences in the rate of infant accidents, hospital referrals, hospital admissions, and contact with emergency departments when comparing psychotic mothers and the control group. The immunization rate in babies was the same in both groups although babies born to psychotic mothers received their immunizations at a later time in their lives.

Clearly, women who are psychotic during pregnancy need extra care during and after the pregnancy. There appears to be a higher risk of neonatal deaths and stillbirths in this population, and women who suffer from psychosis need more encouragement to seek prenatal care as soon as they know they are pregnant, especially if they are already taking antipsychotic medications.

Chapter 9

MEDICATIONS USED FOR
PSYCHOSIS IN PREGNANCY

As mentioned, the atypical antipsychotic medications have shown no increase in birth defects when taken in pregnancy. Other studies on medium-potency or high-potency neuroleptics have shown no increase in risk of taking these medications during pregnancy.

One large study, however, indicated a slightly higher chance of having a congenital anomaly if a woman takes low-potency neuroleptics. Because of this, high-potency agents such as haloperidol (Haldol), perphenazine (Trilafon), and trifluoperazine (Stelazine) have been increasingly recommended over lower-potency medications in treating women in the first trimester of pregnancy with psychotic disorders.

The atypical antipsychotic agents have begun to be used for reasons other than psychosis, such as refractory depression, bipolar disorder, and anxiety disorders. These agents have been studied and found to have a great deal of reproductive safety. Researchers looked at the following agents in a group of more than 150 pregnant women:

- Olanzapine (Zyprexa)
- Risperidone (Risperdal)
- Quetiapine (Seroquel)
- Clozapine (Clozapine)

The study showed no differences among pregnant women taking these drugs and those taking nothing when it came to congenital abnormalities, obstetrical complications, or problems in the newborn. This is a small study, however, and more data needs to be generated.

In order to help identify the possible risks of taking these types of medications, the National Pregnancy Registry (15) has been developed to gain more information on pregnancy and neonatal outcomes in children who have been exposed to these agents in utero. The FDA has also updated the categories for all antipsychotic medications that include various warnings to pregnant mothers who choose to take antipsychotic drugs during pregnancy.

Because pregnancy does not protect a woman from developing a psychiatric disorder and because there are women with existing psychiatric disorders who become pregnant, more research needs to be done in order to identify the various risks in taking medications to treat psychiatric disorders. These need to be weighed against the risks of allowing these women to be untreated during their pregnancy.

As schizophrenic and other psychotic patients have become deinstitutionalized, the fertility rates among these women have gone up. There are more sexual partners and a change in beliefs around women with mental illness having babies. There has been a growth in the use of the second-generation antipsychotic medications (as opposed to first-generation antipsychotics), which have a decreased incidence of elevated prolactin levels, therefore increasing their ability to become pregnant.

Unwanted and unplanned pregnancies occur more often among women with psychosis than in normal women. This can result in a delay in getting prenatal care and the presence of risky behaviors such as alcohol use and the use of illicit drugs.

There is evidence that women who have a psychiatric disorder will worsen their symptoms during the pregnancy (125). Women with bipolar disorder are often in their childbearing years during their illness, so they are also more likely to be pregnant and suffer from bipolar psychosis. They often have worsening of their symptoms during pregnancy, including antidepressant-induced mania, rapid cycling mania, and mixed mania.

Both the first- and second-generation antipsychotics are effective against psychosis in both schizophrenia and other psychoses. Only one study is available, however, on the use of these medications during pregnancy, although the safety of all types of antipsychotic medications has been elucidated by years of use over time (126).

First-generation antipsychotics are less studied than second-generation antipsychotics, but they shouldn't be forgotten as choices in treating psychosis during pregnancy. A single study has been made available on the statistical probabilities of using these low-potency neuroleptic agents during pregnancy (127).

The things looked at regarding the use of antipsychotic medications in pregnancy include the following:

- The chance for major fetal birth defects
- The potential risk to the mother-infant bond with early and late pregnancy exposure to antipsychotic medications
- Neonatal toxicity causing postnatal complications
- Postnatal behavioral issues
- Pregnancy complications

I hear sounds or voices when no one is around.

—Pregnant woman

Antipsychotic Use in Pregnancy

The following are some common second-generation antipsychotic medications often used in pregnancy:

- Aripiprazole (Abilify) is rated FDA Pregnancy Category C. It means that there is evidence of risk to the fetus, but the benefits of use in pregnancy may outweigh the risks. In animal studies, aripiprazole has shown decreased fetal weight, developmental toxicity, and some teratogenic effects when taking doses of three to ten times the maximum recommended dose for humans (129). In two cases, the baby had no structural birth defects, nor did they have impairment of their neurodevelopment. There were some brief symptoms related to neonatal adaptation, but these were resolved without treatment. In a third human case, the fetus was born healthy. In two of the three cases found, the fetus was only exposed to the medication after twenty weeks' gestation.
- Clozapine (Clozaril) has been rated FDA Pregnancy Category B, even though there is little research evidence to support its safety. It has been studied in rabbits and rats at doses of two to four times the normal human dosage with no harm found to the fetus (130). In human studies, the safety of this drug in pregnancy has been studied since the early 1990s. There have been isolated cases of gestational metabolic issues, major birth defects, perinatal adverse reactions, and poor pregnancy outcome

with the taking of clozapine at different stages of the pregnancy, but these were just case reports or studies on small numbers of women. It has been found that clozapine overdose in pregnancy may fatally injure the fetus.

• Olanzapine (Zyprexa) has been ranked FDA Pregnancy Category C. Studies on reproduction and olanzapine have shown no evidence of harm to the fetus in animals (131). Large studies on pregnant women taking olanzapine are, however, lacking. There is a postmarketing surveillance study on more than 8,800 women that revealed a limited number of olanzapine-exposed pregnancies. There was one case of abortion because of a fetal malformation found in utero. The manufacturer has not reported any fetal abnormalities in their databases, but there have been some cases of problems in pregnancy and complicated fetal outcomes after exposing the fetus to olanzapine during pregnancy (132). There have been isolated cases of major birth defects, but according to the manufacturer, this prevalence doesn't differ from that seen in a regular population of pregnant mothers. Even so, a few cases of olanzapine causing birth defects, worsening or onset of gestational diabetes, brief neurodevelopmental issues, and neonatal adverse reactions have been reported. Olanzapine has found to cross the placental barrier to a higher degree than some other antipsychotic medications (133). Even so, there are many reports of healthy pregnancy outcomes among fetuses exposed to olanzapine during various stages of pregnancy.

• Quetiapine (Seroquel) is rated FDA Pregnancy Category C. There has been no teratogenic effects in using quetiapine in animals. In human research, it has been found that quetiapine had the lowest amount of passage through the placental barrier at 23.8 percent compared with haloperidol, risperidone, and olanzapine. There are also no changes in the pharmacokinetics of taking this drug during pregnancy (134). There have been several case reports that have shown healthy pregnancy outcomes among babies who were exposed to quetiapine during the pregnancy. Some of these women were also exposed to other psychotropic medications during their pregnancies. In spite of some case reports of birth defects occurring when using quetiapine during pregnancy, there was no recurrent pattern of birth defects noted. In one study (135), thirty-six psychotic women were given quetiapine in early pregnancy. The outcome of interest was the presence of birth defects as well as pregnancy outcomes and infant outcomes. In the study, quetiapine was unassociated with any type of teratogenic risk, and the health of the mother and infant were found to be normal when compared with controls.

• Risperidone (Risperdal) is classified FDA Pregnancy Category C and has shown no evidence of birth defects in animal studies (136). In humans, the ability of risperidone to cross the placental barrier was 49.2 percent. One study showed reassuring results, indicating no birth defects or pregnancy complications similar to the manufacturer's findings. Only a few clinical studies have shown birth defects and poor pregnancy outcomes when using the drug (137). These studies have been confounded by the fact that many of these women also took other psychotropic drugs, some of which were known to be teratogenic. The conclusion seems to be that there is no increased risk of spontaneous abortions or birth defects in women taking risperidone in pregnancy alone.

• Sertindole (Serdolect and Serlec) is rated Pregnancy Category C by the FDA. There is no human data available on sertindole in pregnancy; however, there have been no increases in birth defects among animal reproductive studies (138).

• Ziprasidone (Geodon) is rated at Pregnancy Category C by the FDA. Animal studies showed developmental toxicity, including an increase in ventricular septal defects and renal birth defects. This was done at doses approaching the human therapeutic dosage (139). There are no data on women taking the drug in pregnancy.

Data on first-generation antipsychotics also exist. These include the following medications:

• Haloperidol (Haldol) has been rated Pregnancy Category C by the FDA. Animal studies failed to demonstrate any birth defects associated with its use (140). In humans, it has been shown to pass the placental barrier by 65.5 percent. There has been information on the use of haloperidol causing limb defects and other birth defects available since 1966. The safety of haloperidol in one study has recently been tested (141). Babies who were exposed to haloperidol in the womb had rates of birth defects well within the expected risk in the normal population. Alternatively, there is warning information on the risk of perinatal adverse reactions in neonates despite a case of drug overdose in which a transient complication was observed in the newborn (142). Some complications noted were an increase in gestational diabetes, feeding and respiratory issues, hypotonia, arrhythmia, and irritability.

• Penfluridol and pimozide (Orap) are both ranked as having an FDA Pregnancy Category C. There were a small number of pregnancies studied, and only one case of fetal malformation was noted. There were no anecdotal cases of birth defects found in human pregnancies (143). This medication is even more potent than Haldol.

• Chlorprothixene (Cloxan, Taractan, and Truxal) and zuclopenthixol (Cisordinol, Clopixol, and Acuphase). Both of these drugs were rated FDA Pregnancy Category C. In some studies, pregnancies examined retrospectively showed some cases of congenital malformations, and gestational diabetes were found in pregnancies exposed to these drugs (144).

- Phenothiazines (Chlorpromazine, Promethazine, and Thioridazine) have been found to be teratogenic in both rats and mice (145). It is not known how or if these drugs cross the placental barrier. In one study (146), a relatively large number of pregnancies involving phenothiazines were studied, especially chlorpromazine-exposed pregnancies. Some fetal birth defects were noted, but these were not higher than the rate in unexposed women. There was, however, a high rate of spontaneous miscarriages in the study at 23.4 percent. There was a statistically significant increase in the rate of major congenital anomalies among certain phenothiazines (chlorpromazine, methotrimeprazine, trimeprazine, and oxomemazine). Because phenothiazine drugs were also used to control the threat of miscarriage, the early pregnancy losses may have been due to a previous chromosomal abnormality (147). There also seemed to be an increased chance of developing neonatal jaundice in babies who were preterm and who had mothers taking phenothiazines during the labor process. A single study looked at the long-term behavioral effects among children exposed to phenothiazines after twenty weeks' gestation (148). The children studied were between the ages of nine and ten years and showed no changes in their behavior when compared with controls.

- Chlorpromazine (Thorazine) is rated at Pregnancy Category C by the FDA. In animal studies, it has been associated with a greater risk of cleft palate, CNS defects, eye defects, skeletal defects, fetal demise, and decreased fetal weight gain. The doses of chlorpromazine used were many times greater than the recommended dose in humans (149). In studies of a small number of psychotic women in pregnancy, there were no abnormal findings in the babies after first-trimester exposure to chlorpromazine. So far, only one case of birth defects and gestational diabetes has been reported. Perinatal complications seem to be a common finding whenever the drug is used in the latter parts of the pregnancy (150).

- Prochlorperazine (Compazine, Stemzine, Buccastem, Stemetil, and Phenotil) is rated at a FDA Pregnancy Category C. One case of a fatal fetal anomaly was found in a woman who needed prochlorperazine to treat hyperemesis gravidarum (151). Other case reports have shown an increased chance of having both major and minor birth defects after exposing the mother to prochlorperazine in the first twenty weeks of pregnancy. This has been refuted in other studies, which showed no cases of fetal birth defects after a large number of women who used prochlorperazine in pregnancy were studied.

- Trifluoperazine (Stelazine) is ranked at FDA Pregnancy Category C. The manufacturer, Smith, Kline, and French, took a look at its database in order to decide if there was evidence of a relationship between the use trifluoperazine in pregnancy and a risk of birth defects (152). They found no risk in taking the drug during pregnancy. Most women took the drug for nausea and vomiting during pregnancy (87 percent), while 13 percent of women who took the drug for a psychiatric disorder. In December of 1992, the Canadian Food and Drug Directorate came out with a statement that the use of trifluoperazine in pregnancy may be linked to sporadic cases of congenital birth defects, including many types of internal malformations and skeletal defects (153). Overall, however, the results have been mixed.

- Fluphenazine (Prolixin) has not been assigned a pregnancy category by the FDA. Most of the studies on the use of this drug involved women who used the medication for hyperemesis gravidarum. The rates of miscarriage, perinatal mortality, fetal birth defects, and premature delivery were the same as with women who took a placebo drug (154). There have been occasional case reports and information from birth registers which have shown the relative safety of taking fluphenazine during pregnancy. The use of the drug also rarely resulted in metabolic complications but may have caused some adverse effects in the newborn.

- Thioridazine (Mellaril) has not been assigned a pregnancy category. One study on a small number of women who used low doses of thioridazine in pregnancy showed no birth complications (155). Exposure in utero, however, may be linked to a greater risk of extrapyramidal symptoms in newborns. There has only been one case of fetal birth defects following in utero exposure to thioridazine.

- Promethazine (Phenergan), perphenazine (Trilafon), and levomepromazine (Nosinan, Nozinan, and Levoprome) are rated Pregnancy Category C. With promethazine, a relatively large number of women exposed in early pregnancy have been studied. The rate of major birth defects was 4.3 percent, which did not differ from the expected rate of birth defects (156). There were two reports in which birth defects were identified in infants exposed in utero to perphenazine, but they also took amitriptyline during early pregnancy. There were occasional case reports of birth defects and gestational diabetes in women who took perphenazine in pregnancy, but these didn't seem to be above the normal rate of birth defects.

*I feel that my thoughts are not my own and that
they are totally out of my control.*

—*Woman with tough thought*

Guidelines for Use

There have been published guidelines that have highlighted the necessity in starting or continuing antipsychotic therapy in high-risk mothers because the risk of relapse or recurrence of psychotic symptoms can, in and of themselves, result in medical or obstetrical complications. These guidelines weren't very helpful because they provided no information on the use of antipsychotics with the belief that there wasn't much information on the use of antipsychotics in pregnancy, and they weren't considered safe.

Majority of the studies on the safety of antipsychotic drugs in pregnancy were characterized by experimental designs that were unable to tease out all the various factors affecting psychotic pregnant mothers that were independent of drug use, such as malnutrition, poor prenatal care, sexual violence, domestic violence, sexually transmitted diseases, and other unhealthy behaviors (157).

Studies also have had their limitations. It is unethical, for example, to include pregnant mothers to drugs in randomized controlled trials because these would involve the deliberate exposure of fetuses to drugs that are potentially teratogenic. As a result, the best data on the use of antipsychotic drugs in pregnancy come from nonrandomized, prospective, and observational studies. There have been single case reports or reports on a small number of women.

In the absence of more controlled studies, the reviewed studies available have provided us with the only information useful in clinical practice in treating pregnant mothers with psychosis.

As a whole, antipsychotic medications have been associated with an increase in the chances of having birth defects in the fetus, but there have been no differences in birth defect risk between the various classes of medications or with specific medications. This means that there may be underlying pathology associated with being psychotic that may explain the increased risk of birth defects rather than the medications.

The use of both first-generation and second-generation antipsychotic medications has been associated with a greater risk of perinatal complications. When it comes to the teratogenic risk of ziprasidone, sertindole, and amisulpride, the risk should be considered unknown. Only three cases have been found using aripiprazole; one of these studies showed temporary changes in the newborn's cardiac rhythm. For these reasons, these drugs should be avoided in pregnancy because the data are poor, or there is limited anecdotal data available regarding their teratogenicity.

About two hundred babies have been studied who were exposed to clozapine while in the womb. There were fifteen cases of birth defects as well as poor pregnancy outcomes and complications in the newborn. The main complications were retinopathy, transient floppy infant syndrome, and severe newborn hypoxemic encephalopathy. In most of the cases, however, no information was given on the type of birth defect found so that patterns of birth defects could not be obtained.

In some instances, the pregnant mothers took other medications besides antipsychotics. One study raised the possibility of fetal agranulocytosis among infants exposed to clozapine (158). This means that the WBC should be evaluated in all newborns who have been exposed to clozapine during the pregnancy and should be monitored every week for the first six months of life in order to detect the presence of agranulocytosis that might cause life-threatening infections in the infant.

Second-Generation Antipsychotic Guidelines

Olanzapine (Zyprexa) is the second-generation antipsychotic (SGA) with the highest number of reports regarding it being given in pregnancy, with the number of cases being 419 women. Any attempt to check on the teratogenicity of olanzapine has been complicated by the fact that these women were also exposed to other psychotropic drugs. Twenty-six cases of congenital defects have been reported, including neural tube defects in four of the cases (159). This might suggest that the drug may cause a specific birth defect. Sixty-three cases of postpartum complications following exposure to olanzapine in pregnancy have been reported.

More than two hundred reports of pregnancies exposed to quetiapine are currently available, with birth defects found in eight cases. Because the number of cases is so small, no conclusions can be drawn regarding the safety of this drug in early pregnancy.

There are more than three hundred cases of in utero exposure to risperidone available. There were fifteen cases of birth defects, but no recurrent patterns emerged. Perinatal complications of various degrees of severity can also happen, ranging from withdrawal reactions to seizures in the neonate (160). There have also been rare cases of poor pregnancy outcomes and complications in the newborn.

Most second-generation antipsychotic medications (except aripiprazole and ziprasidone) are likely to induce obesity and other metabolic complications in the mother. The risk is highest among women in their childbearing years. Women who are obese before their pregnancy are more likely to deliver babies with birth defects than those women who are not obese.

Gestational diabetes has been associated with an increased risk of coming down with breast cancer in later life. Infants exposed to second-generation antipsychotics have an increased risk of being large for gestational age when compared with first-generation antipsychotics (161). These infants can suffer from newborn hypoglycemia as well as decreased insulin sensitivity at birth, obesity, heart disease, and diabetes in their later life.

The two drugs, clozapine and olanzapine, should be considered the highest risk for metabolic complications in the pregnant mother, primarily gestational diabetes. On the other hand, the other antipsychotics have not been associated with gestational diabetic complications, with only one case found in risperidone use.

First-Generation Antipsychotics (FGA) Guidelines

Despite more than forty years of use and a reasonably extensive safety database, there are only about four hundred cases of pregnancies associated with the use of haloperidol. Overall, about fourteen cases of birth defects were noted, of which three were limb abnormalities (162). This means that limb abnormalities from early exposure in utero to haloperidol cannot be ruled out. There have also been cases of late in utero exposure to haloperidol resulting in withdrawal symptoms.

A relatively large number of cases of babies exposed to phenothiazine agents have been investigated (more than four thousand cases). Most of these babies were exposed to these types of agents for only a short period of time, and most of the mothers took the drugs for hyperemesis gravidarum. Because of this, little information about the dangers of taking specific drugs can be made available. The overall rate of birth defects was around 10 percent.

First-generation antipsychotic medications also cause weight gain with long-term treatment. Early exposure to chlorpromazine and thioxanthenes have been associated with the onset or worsening of gestational diabetes in pregnant mothers.

Treatment with Antipsychotics in Pregnancy

Even though there is a definite lack of safety data on antipsychotic medications, the use of these medications should be considered mandatory in women with psychotic disorders during pregnancy because the risks associated with giving these medications outweigh the risks of having an untreated mental illness in the mother (163).

It should be noted that most of these pregnant mothers require admission to a psychiatric unit for the pharmacological management of psychotic breakdown episodes. In such instances, antipsychotics are the most commonly used medications (164). Some psychotic women seem to have an independent risk factor for an adverse pregnancy outcome, such as medical problems in the mother, eclampsia, placental anomalies, preterm labor, low Apgar scores, low birth weight, hemorrhages during birth, fetal distress, birth defects, and perinatal mortality.

It should also be highlighted that things like low birth weight and increased rates of suicide among the offspring as they get older are also important. This seems to be especially true among schizophrenics, who already have an increased risk of having small-for-gestational-age infants, infants with neurological defects and low birth weight, and preterm birth.

The increase in pregnancy complications among schizophrenic mothers seems to be related to the increase in risky behaviors among these mothers in pregnancy. Genetic susceptibility to schizophrenia, on the other hand, doesn't appear to influence the natural course of the woman's pregnancy (165).

Regardless, women with psychotic disorders can have a devastating impact on the quality of the mother-infant bonding and on the infant's development. Mothers who have schizophrenia are more likely to have their attachment to the baby harmed by their psychopathology and the reality of their psychosocial situation. These women are more likely to have problems with parenting and are therefore more likely to lose custody of their babies. Maternal bipolar disorder has been associated with an increase in the rates of memory disturbances, attention disturbances, behavioral problems, emotional problems, and psychiatric disorders in children (166).

Sometimes, doctors need to manage psychotic symptoms in pregnant women who have not taken any type of antipsychotic drug in the past. In such cases, the first-generation antipsychotics should be preferred. Chlorpromazine should be a first-line agent because it has less worrisome teratogenic effects.

In general, the guidelines should include the following:

- When a planned or unplanned pregnancy occurs when a woman is on an antipsychotic therapy, the drug should be continued as pregnancy is not the best time to experiment with the effectiveness of another drug.
- Antipsychotic therapy should be mandatory in pregnant moms with psychosis.
- In the case of a new onset psychosis, the drug of choice should be one in which there is the least degree of teratogenicity, such as chlorpromazine.
- The Hemoglobin A1c should be monitored along with body weight and cholesterol/triglyceride levels in women taking antipsychotic medication.
- Strict surveillance should be undertaken with both first- and second-generation antipsychotics.

- Consideration should be made to taper off the antipsychotic medication during the last trimester in order to reduce the risk of neonatal extrapyramidal symptoms and seizures as long as the risk of psychotic relapse is minimal.
- There should be cooperation between the obstetrician, neonatologist, and pediatrician so as to have adequate prenatal care and promptly diagnose and manage any types of complications occurring during the first few hours after the birth.
- The children born to these mothers should have regular follow-up in order to manage any signs of neurodevelopmental problems.

Conclusion

Psychotic women wish to have children, and as many as 50 percent of them are mothers, which nearly equals that of the normal population. These women should have drug management of their underlying illness, and this should be part of a multidisciplinary approach. Various tools should be used and implemented before conception in order to reduce risky behavior that might contribute to an increase in birth defects, such as drug use, smoking, and alcohol use, as well as unprotected sexual activities.

The main concern of pregnant women with psychosis is a probable psychotic relapse because of nonadherence to neuroleptic medications, which can lead to termination of the pregnancy, cesarean section, and institutionalization of the children because of reduced child care availability. For this reason, doctors should make all possible effort to inform psychotic mothers about the advantage of taking on a modest increase in birth defects in order to maintain a stable mental health status during pregnancy.

Another tool that should be used is the enhancement of all other non–drug related support programs for the mother. Steps should be taken to prevent attachment turmoil after birth. There should be social support for the mother and the identification of potential caregivers for the child should the mother suffer a relapse after birth.

I am afraid I might harm myself in order to escape this pain

—Pregnant heroin user

Chapter 10

OPOID DEPENDANCE IN PREGNANCY

Women take opioids in pregnancy for a number of reasons. These include taking opioids for pain relief (analgesia), cough suppression, euphoria, or sedation. There are true opioids, such as codeine and morphine, and semisynthetic opioids, such as Vicodin (containing hydrocodone), Percocet (containing oxycodone), and heroin. True synthetic opioids include methadone (Dolophine) and fentanyl (Duragesic and Sublamaze).

Heroin use is especially problematic in pregnancy. It is a white- or brown-colored powder that is dissolved in water and injected intravenously, although it can be taken by other routes. Common street names for heroin and other opiates include the following:

- Junk, H, big H, smack, horse, skag, dope, shit, hell dust
- Nose drops (liquefied heroin)
- Dragon rock (heroin mixed with cocaine)
- A bomb (heroin mixed with marijuana)
- M, morph, Miss Emma, monkey, Roxanol, white stuff (morphine)
- Juice, meth (methadone)
- Vikes, hydro, Norcos (hydromorphone)
- Oxy, OC, Percs (Oxycodone)

Opioid use is prevalent. There are currently about 810,000 to one million chronic heroin users in the United States and about 6.4 million people who abuse prescription narcotics. About 3.8 million Americans (twelve years of age and older) have reported using heroin at least once in their lifetime. The problem has intensified as the price has decreased and the purity has increased. The purity of heroin in 1970 was about 10 percent. This has increased to 50–80 percent in the

1990s. The overdose potential is also great, especially when the individual tries to quit opioids and goes back to the dose they took before they quit taking opioids.

Women at Risk for Opioid Use

There are some women who carry a higher risk of opioid abuse compared with others because of the following reasons:

- Being unemployed
- Suffering from poverty
- Having poor working conditions
- Having poor coping skills and lack of personal health skills
- Having a hereditary predisposition to taking opioids
- Lack of education and literacy skills
- Lack of social support
- Lack of healthcare access
- Living in an environment where the use of substances numb the woman to life's realities

The short-term effects of taking heroin include the following:

- Dry mouth
- Warm flushing of the skin
- Heaviness of the arms and legs
- Slowed gait
- Impaired night vision
- Droopy eyelids

Pregnant women can suffer withdrawal effects from stopping heroin acutely. These include symptoms that begin within hours of stopping the heroin and peak at two to three days. They are largely resolved within five to ten days. Common psychological symptoms include insomnia, anxiety, and cravings for the drug, which can last for many weeks or even months. Most women describe the psychological symptoms as being far worse than the physical symptoms experienced as part of heroin withdrawal. Withdrawal can put a woman at risk for suicidality and overdose if they start taking the drug again.

Maternal consequences of long-term use of heroin include bacterial endocarditis and infection of the heart valves; pneumonia; blood clots in the arteries leading to the lung, liver, kidney, or brain; physical addiction; increased tolerance; liver disease; and death. Women who take heroin are also at higher risk of the following:

- Anemia
- Heart disease
- Pneumonia
- Hepatitis
- Diabetes
- HIV
- Cellulitis

In pregnancy, heroin addiction can lead to maternal and fetal malnutrition, small-for-gestational-age infants, bleeding in the third trimester, preterm labor, fetal HIV disease, childhood behavioral abnormalities, neonatal abstinence syndrome, neonatal death, and mental retardation. The rate of birth defects is about 2–3 percent, with some infants developing congenital heart defects, spina bifida, hydrocephaly, hypoxic ischemic brain injury, glaucoma, gastroschisis, and prolonged QT syndrome.

Risks of Opioid Use in Pregnancy

The use of illicit opioid drugs in pregnancy has been linked to adverse outcomes. Abruptly stopping opioids in a woman who is pregnant and is opioid dependent can cause an increased risk of fetal distress, preterm labor, and fetal death. While the woman is pregnant and during the postpartum state, doctors need to take on special considerations to ensure pain management is achieved and to prevent relapse after the baby is born or overdoses when opioids are started again after delivery.

Opioid use in pregnancy involves both the use of heroin and the abuse of prescription opioid analgesic pills. According to the 2010 National Survey on Drug Use and Health, approximately 4.4 percent of women who are pregnant reported taking some type of illicit drug within the past thirty days (45). The use of opioid analgesics is higher than the rate of heroin use during pregnancy. One percent of pregnant women used opioid analgesics in pregnancy versus 0.1 percent of women who used heroin in pregnancy (46). The urine screening of pregnant women in an urban hospital setting yielded somewhat higher results, with 2.6 percent testing positive for opioids. Because this prevalence is relatively high, doctors who deliver babies must be aware of the potential for opioid use among pregnant women as well of the proper management techniques.

Opioid addiction results from the repetitive use of prescription opioids or heroin. Heroin is the most rapidly acting of all opioids and thus is highly addictive. Heroin, as mentioned, is usually taken intravenously, but it can be nasally inhaled or smoked. It has a short half-life, so many doses need to be taken each day to achieve long-lasting effects.

Prescribed opioid medications are also abused. They may be injected, swallowed, inhaled through the nose, chewed, taken as a suppository, or smoked. The onset of action varies according to the way the drug was taken and the type of medication used. Injection of these drugs carry the risk of abscess formation or cellulitis at the site of injection, endocarditis, sepsis, osteomyelitis, hepatitis C, hepatitis B, and HIV.

Opioids bind to opioid receptors within the brain, producing euphoria. They also depress respirations, leading to respiratory arrest and subsequent death. There is a great degree of tolerance in opioid addiction, so the user needs to take higher doses to achieve the same effect. Once physical dependence to the drug has occurred, there are significant withdrawal symptoms once the drug is stopped. With heroin, withdrawal symptoms can occur within four to six hours, and they don't subside until a week after the last use.

For long-acting opioid medications (like methadone), withdrawal symptoms begin about twenty-four hours to thirty-six hours of use and can last for several weeks. Drug cravings and obsessing about the drug can last for several years, increasing the risk of relapsing. While withdrawal from heroin is not considered fatal to normal, healthy adults, fetal death is possible in pregnant women who are not treated for opioid addiction because of the risk of acute opioid abstinence syndrome (47). There is an association between using codeine in the first trimester of pregnancy and the risk of congenital heart defects in infants. Other reports are contradictory, showing no increase in birth defects when a woman has taken oxycodone, meperidine, or propoxyphene during pregnancy (48). The observed congenital anomalies are still quite rare with a small increase in the absolute risk compared with those who didn't take opioids.

During pregnancy, chronic heroin use has been associated with a greater risk of placental abruption, intrauterine growth retardation, preterm labor, fetal death, and meconium at the time of birth. The effects may be due to the drug itself or the repeated withdrawal that can occur with the use of this drug. Lifestyle issues also come into play. The things a woman does to support her habit, such as prostitution, violence, and theft, put her at risk of sustaining violence upon herself, loss of custody of the child, criminal cases, and time in jail.

Screening for Opioid Abuse in Pregnancy

Screening for the use of substances should be part of complete prenatal care and should be done as a partnership with the pregnant woman. Women should be asked about their use of both alcohol and drugs before they get pregnant as well as in early pregnancy. The woman should be made aware that these types of questions are asked of all pregnant women to assure the health of the woman and her unborn fetus, and they should be told that all information is to be kept confidential. A caring and nonjudgmental approach should be used in order to get the most information from the mother. There are screening tools that can be used to identify those who are using illicit drugs.

Besides screening tools, doctors need to be aware of certain signs and symptoms that suggest substance use is present in pregnant women. Late onset of prenatal care, failing appointments, poor weight gain, signs of intoxication, signs of sedation, erratic behavior, and evidence of withdrawal are things a doctor should look for.

The physical examination should entail looking for tell-tale track marks from IV drug use, skin lesions from intra-dermal injections, abscesses, and cellulitis—all indicators of IV or intradermal drug use. Urine drug testing can be performed if drug use is suspected, but it must be used with the pregnant woman's consent. There may be ramifications of a positive result, including requirements for mandatory reporting (49).

Clinical Screening Tools for Substance Abuse in Pregnancy

One clinical screening tool involves the use of the "4 Ps" in which the following questions are asked:

- Parents. "Did any of your parents have a problem with alcohol or other drug use?"
- Partner. "Does your partner have a problem with alcohol or drug use?"
- Past. "In the past, have you had difficulties in your life because of alcohol or other drugs, including prescription medications?"
- Present. "In the past month, have you drunk any alcohol or used other drugs?"
  A "yes" answer to any of these questions should prompt further investigation on current drug use in pregnancy (50).
  Another good screening tool for drug use in pregnancy is the CRAFFT Screening Tool. This involves asking the following questions:
- Have you ever ridden in a car driven by someone (including yourself) who was high or who had been using alcohol or drugs?
- Do you ever use alcohol or drugs to relax, feel better about yourself, or fit in?
- Do you ever use alcohol or drugs while you are by yourself or alone?
- Do you ever forget things you did while using alcohol or drugs?
- Do family or friends ever tell you that you should cut down on your drinking or drug use?
- Have you ever gotten into trouble while you were using alcohol or drugs?

A score of two positive items or more indicates that the doctor should investigate further for drug use in the pregnant mother (51).

An opioid antagonist, such as naloxone, should never be used to diagnose opioid dependence in pregnant women because it could induce a withdrawal state that can precipitate fetal distress or preterm labor. Instead, it should only be used in cases of maternal overdose, in which it would be used to save the woman's and fetus's lives (52).

Chapter 11

TREATMENT OF OPOID DEPENDANCE

Methadone has been used since the 1970s as maintenance therapy for pregnant women addicted to heroin. It has recently been used for the management of nonheroin opioid dependence as well.

The rationale behind using methadone during pregnancy has been to reduce the complications of heroin use and narcotic withdrawal. It also encourages adequate prenatal care and treatment for drug dependence. It reduces criminal activity on the mother's part and helps her avoid the risks to the patient of associating with those in the drug culture from which she came. Taking methadone doesn't prevent neonatal abstinence syndrome; however, this is treatable when used in collaboration with the pediatrician caring for the infant.

The use of methadone (dispensed on a daily basis) becomes part of a total package that includes prenatal care, counseling on chemical dependency, nutritional education, and family therapy, as well as other services needed for pregnant women suffering from opioid dependency. Methadone dosages are managed by addiction specialists within registered methadone programs.

Obstetricians and family doctors should talk to the addiction treatment program if concerns are raised about the mother's overall care and her methadone dose. The dose needs to be adjusted during the pregnancy to avoid the occurrence of withdrawal symptoms, such as abdominal cramps, cravings for the drug, insomnia, anxiety, irritability, nausea, and insomnia. If the woman is already on methadone prior to her pregnancy, it should be known that there are pharmacokinetic effects that require an adjustment in dosage during the latter part of the pregnancy.

The usual dose of methadone is about 10–30 mg per day. If treatment is begun while a woman is pregnant, the dosage should be titrated until she becomes asymptomatic. If the dosage of methadone is inadequate, withdrawal symptoms can occur, which can cause fetal distress and can increase the chances of a relapse into using heroin or other opioids again.

As mentioned, neonatal abstinence syndrome still occurs with methadone treatments. The severity of these withdrawal symptoms in the neonate is probably not associated with the actual dose of methadone the mother is on (53).

A pregnant woman should be advised to begin methadone induction using a licensed outpatient methadone program. In situations where the woman needs to be hospitalized in order to begin taking methadone, there should be arrangements prior to discharge to send her to an outpatient drug addiction program as soon as she is discharged. It is illegal for a physician to write a prescription for methadone outside of a licensed treatment program (54).

Buprenorphine (Suboxone, Subutex) can be prescribed in an office-based setting by accredited physicians who have undertaken a specific credentialing program. Doctors need to be familiar with the state and federal guidelines regarding the prescribing of the various medications used in the treatment of opioid abuse.

Buprenorphine is considered a good choice for the treatment of opioid dependence in pregnancy. It binds to the same receptors as morphine and heroin and can be used as part of the treatment plan in women suffering from opioid dependence, provided they know the risks and benefits (55).

There are advantages to using buprenorphine instead of methadone. These include a reduced risk of overdose, the ability to be treated as an outpatient, the lack of the need to visit a licensed treatment program on a daily basis, and fewer drug interactions. The neonatal abstinence syndrome is less severe as well. Unfortunately, there is a risk of hepatic dysfunction, no evidence of long-term complications in the infant, and a higher dropout rate because of dissatisfaction with taking the drug. The woman also has the ability to sell her prescribed buprenorphine to others.

Buprenorphine can be given alone or in combination with naloxone (Narcan), which reduces the chances she will sell the drug. It also prevents the injection of the drug because it can cause severe withdrawal effects if injected. In pregnancy, buprenorphine (Subutex) alone is recommended in order to avoid exposure of the fetus to naloxone (Narcan) if the combined drug is injected. The Substance Abuse and Mental Health Services Administration has a published accounting of all physicians who are licensed to prescribe buprenorphine.

Until very recently, data on the use of buprenorphine in pregnant women have been scarce. One study was done in 2010 (56) comparing the risks of neonatal abstinence syndrome in women who took buprenorphine versus methadone. A total of 175 opioid-addicted pregnant women were studied. In the study, newborns needed about 89 percent less morphine, had a 58 percent shorter duration of treatment, and had a 43 percent shorter hospital stay when taking buprenorphine for neonatal abstinence syndrome.

If a pregnant woman is already receiving methadone for her opioid dependence, buprenorphine should not be used because there is a greater risk of withdrawal when the switch is made.

Withdrawing completely from opioids during pregnancy is not advised because there is a high relapse rate associated with withdrawing from these drugs. If methadone is unavailable or if the woman refuses to take buprenorphine or methadone, a medically supervised withdrawal from opiates should be done in the second trimester and only under the supervision of a doctor who has experience in this type of withdrawal.

Perinatal and Postpartum Management of Opioid-Dependent Women

Women should receive opiates in labor just as if she were not taking opiates already because the medications used for maintenance are not in a high-enough dose to provide adequate analgesia for labor (57). Narcotics that are also antagonists should not be used because they can precipitate withdrawal in labor. Buprenorphine should not be given to a methadone-taking woman. The pediatrician and staff should be notified of the impending birth of an infant exposed to narcotics.

Patients taking opioid maintenance therapy will need higher doses of analgesia in labor. In one study, women who had a Cesarean section and who took buprenorphine during the pregnancy needed 47 percent more opioid medication than women who did not take buprenorphine (58). Injectable NSAIDs like ketorolac were also found to be effective in controlling postoperative pain. Regular doses of buprenorphine or methadone should be given in labor in order to prevent withdrawal symptoms.

Women who plan to breast-feed should know that there are minimal amounts of buprenorphine and methadone secreted in breast milk regardless of dose. Breast-feeding should be allowed as long as the woman is not HIV-positive. Swaddling during breast-feeding can lessen the symptoms of neonatal abstinence syndrome. Breast-feeding also encourages bonding between the mother and her baby.

While some women will need more methadone and buprenorphine during the pregnancy, others will not. For those who had an increase in dose during pregnancy, they should be watched carefully after delivery for signs of oversedation (59). There should always be access to social and psychological support for these women as they leave the hospital with their babies.

Neonatal Abstinence Syndrome (NAS)

The neonate is still at risk for neonatal abstinence syndrome, even when the mother is taking buprenorphine or methadone. Infants with this syndrome have poor sucking reflexes, poor feeding, irritability, and a high-pitched cry. In infants who have been exposed to methadone, the symptoms usually begin within three days of birth and can last for up to two weeks. Infants who were exposed to buprenorphine, on the other hand, begin to have symptoms about twelve to forty-eight hours after birth with resolution of symptoms after a week (60). Treatment is considered no longer necessary when the infant is able to feed normally, is gaining weight, and has a normal sleep pattern.

About 40–60 percent of newborns experience neonatal abstinence syndrome when the mother has taken heroin during pregnancy. The risk is about 85 percent among mothers who took methadone as part of the treatment of heroin addiction. Withdrawal is usually more severe if the mother is taking benzodiazepines or alcohol along with opiates. About 30–50 percent of neonates will need some kind of pharmacological treatment to handle neonatal abstinence syndrome.

Measures that help manage NAS in the neonate include swaddling the infant, providing a quiet environment, providing "kangaroo care," stimulating the infant minimally, and giving small but frequent doses of short-acting opiates such as morphine that are gradually tapered off over several days to weeks after the symptoms develop. These infants need to be hospitalized for a minimum of ninety-six hours with monitoring of their cardiorespiratory state and pulse oximetry.

In the immediate postpartum period, naloxone should be avoided during the resuscitation process because it can precipitate seizures in the infant. The baby will be assessed using standard scoring systems, and urine can be obtained for toxicology in guiding the treatment of NAS.

Long-Term Infant Outcome when the Mother Was Opioid Addicted

There is very little data on the long-term outcome of babies born to opioid-addicted mothers. Most studies have not found any differences in cognitive functioning in children studied up to five years of age who were exposed to methadone in the womb when compared with control groups (61). Other studies have shown that these children have reduced height and weight compared with control groups, as well as impaired behavior and problems with perceptual and organizational difficulties. Even so, these children should be exposed to preventative interventions that enrich their early childhood experiences.

Chapter 12

SCREENING FOR POSTPARTUM DEPRESSION

It is now common practice to screen a postpartum woman for the presence of postpartum depression. It can be done at the six-week postpartum visit or through a phone interview a couple of weeks after the birth of the baby.

Two common screening tools for depression and particularly for postpartum depression are the Beck Depression Inventory and the Edinburgh Postnatal Depression Scale or EPDS. The Beck Depression Inventory is designed to be used in any type of depression, while the Edinburgh Postnatal Depression Scale specifically addresses postnatal depression.

On January 26, the United States Preventative Services Task Force (USPSTF), which sets forth guidelines around preventive and diagnostic screening, announced its recommendation that pregnant and postpartum women should be routinely screened for depression. The USPSTF further recommended that mothers with positive screening results—utilizing such standardized tests as the PHQ-9 or EPDS—should receive additional assessment for the severity of depression, comorbid conditions, and alternative diagnoses. They did not specify an optimal timing for this screening. The American Academy of Pediatricians recommended screening mothers at the infant's one-, two-, and four-month visits. The American College of Obstetricians and Gynecologists recommended screening once during the perinatal period.

The USPSTF, an independent, volunteer panel of national experts in prevention and evidence-based medicine that works to improve the health of all Americans by making evidence-based recommendations about clinical preventive services such as screenings, counseling services, and preventive medications, found convincing evidence that screening for maternal mental health issues (during and after pregnancy) improves accurate identification of adults with depression in primary care settings.

The USPSTF reviewed twenty-three studies using EPDS with a sensitivity of 95 percent and specificity at .90 and using a cutoff score of 13. The Spanish language version also showed acceptable performance characteristics. They felt no other scales (Beck, PHQ) met the inclusion criteria.

Ohio added maternal health screening to the Medicaid fee schedule to pay for the screening. They suggested using the EPDS and Patient Health Questionnaire (PHQ).

Postpartum Risk Assessment in a Suburban Population

The purpose of this study was to identify how many women at childbirth were at risk of perinatal mood disorders for early intervention and the education of mothers and caregivers of how many women were at risk and to involve them at follow-up (either the GYN, the pediatrician, or both). Locally, women are encouraged to stop psychotropic medications early in the pregnancy or in the third trimester to avoid any postdelivery problems in the newborn (jittery baby syndrome). The concern is that this is when women are the most vulnerable to mood disorders, and they are often discouraged from breast-feeding, except when taking sertraline.

All women were given a Postpartum Depression Risk Assessment (PDRA) within twenty-four hours of delivery and were scored. Scales were scored none, moderate, high, or immediate by the number and type of yes responses. Those women scoring high or immediate were seen by the social worker or the psychiatrist. A review of symptoms of risk, psychiatric medication, family histories, and social stressors, as well as a teaching on postpartum mood disorders were conducted. Home-going literature and a list of resources were given to the individual. A letter was sent to the OB/GYN with a copy of the woman's scale and a blank EPDS for follow-up at the six-week postpartum checkup. Women with an immediate score had a letter, a copy of the scale, and an EPDS sent to both the OB/GYN and the pediatrician.

A total of 1,137 PDRA scales were completed, with 70.6 percent scoring none or moderate responses. Twenty-one percent scored high risk, and 6 percent needed immediate intervention at eight months of the study. This correlates well with expected statistics of PPD/mood disorders. There were 148 psychiatric consults completed.

Spectrum Health, based in Grand Rapids, Michigan, has a postpartum support program that started in 2005. There are more than twenty-five hospitals using the PDRA (or similar versions) under the training of Nancy Roberts, RN. They have more than fifty thousand completed assessments. The results were

81

66 percent scoring none or moderate, 25 percent high, and 5 percent immediate, validating the similar ranges of percentages. Their data includes age, race, parity, number of previous miscarriages, type of birth (vaginal versus C-section), preterm labor, type of feeding (bottle versus breast), history of depression, and prior use of antidepressants. They intervene for one-third of their 8,300 new mothers per year.

A copy of the PDRA and a version for neonatal loss are indexed with a copy of the PHQ.

Postpartum Depression in an Inner-city Population

In psychiatry residency training, I went to the OB/GYN residents and suggested they send their depressed patients to me. They stated they did not have any depressed women. They stated the biggest problem was that there was a 50 percent no-show rate at six weeks postpartum checkup, which is when they would have considered looking for depression. Miriam Rosenthal, MD, suggested I study this population, and there were several questions. The first was, why do women in an inner-city population not come for the six-week postpartum check? Is it because they are depressed? Is it because they don't have transportation? Is it just this population of women? So I made a questionnaire that included those questions, as well as completing EPDS, and went to the clinic where the women would have their six-week postpartum check. Using the scheduled appointments, I asked them to complete the evaluation. I mailed a similar questionnaire (wording changed about getting to the clinic) and EPDS to the women who did not come. I followed up with a phone call with both the women who came to the clinic and with those that scored in the clinically depressed scale that did not come to the appointment. As this was my first study, I was not aware of the complications of including a write line in the questionnaire as they are difficult to score. However, that mistake brought valuable information. Among 1,200 women in the clinic and an equivalent number of women who did not show up, I had received approximately 250 complete responses returned in the mail.

The rates of depression was approximately 18 percent using a cutoff score of ten on EPDS. If you used the score of eight, more than 25 percent were depressed. Those that came to the appointments used cars by majority to get to the appointment. One fourteen-year-old responded that she had driven her grandmother's car. The population was predominately African American, and two thirds were married. There was no statistical relevance to parity. What was statistically significant was the younger the patient, the more depressed they were. I had expected women to write in physical ailments in the line of what had bothered them the most since the birth of their baby. What I got back was the baby crying. It became also statistically significant that the younger they were, the more depressed they were. They felt an inability to soothe the infant that contributed to their depression.

I called each woman and invited her to come to an appointment to work on her depression. When I called them, I would state that it looked like, by completing the form, things might be tough with the new baby. They would often respond, "Yeah, I'm just depressed." Not one single woman that I offered a free appointment to work on this problem came to the appointment. More than 50 percent of the phone numbers were no longer correct or had been disconnected.

I was struck by several things in the outcome of this study. Through investigation, I discovered that the postpartum appointments were arbitrarily looked up on the computer and the date handed to the woman at discharge from the hospital without feedback from the client if that was a good time/location for the appointment. At the clinic, I was told by the staff that the mothers were not allowed to have any food items in the waiting area. This was particularly problematic for mothers who had more than one baby because that meant no snacks, juice, or bottles for the toddlers, or children who accompanied them. There were also no items for the children to play with because the staff was unwilling to wash them. I offered to go to garage sales to collect books and distribute them to the children but was told that would be too large of a mess. The women in the waiting area often appeared to be depressed, frustrated with the children they had with them, and irritable. Some were apathetic. The toddlers were clearly unable to just sit and wait, and often the waiting area was filled with babies and children crying. One young woman sat in the corner with her head down, which she had shaved, with the infant wailing loudly at her feet. I offered to hold the baby while she completed the questionnaire. I offered crayons to use on the backs of questionnaires to the toddlers as mothers completed the questionnaire.

Edinburgh Postnatal Depression Scale

The EPDS is a scale that measures postpartum depression with a reasonable degree of accuracy. A woman who scores high for postpartum depression on this scale is then referred for further evaluation and management of postpartum depression. The EPDS is simply a screening tool designed to identify those mothers who are at a higher risk for depression after delivery. The EPDS is as follows:

"As you are pregnant or have recently had a baby, we would like to know how you are feeling. Please check the answer that comes closest to how you have felt in the past seven days, not just how you feel today."

1. I have been able to laugh and see the funny side of things.
   o As much as I always could
   o Not quite as much now
   o Definitely not so much now
   o I haven't been coping as well at all

2. I have looked forward with enjoyment to things.
   o As much as I ever did
   o Rather less than I used to
   o Definitely less than I used to
   o Hardly at all

3. I have blamed myself unnecessarily when things went wrong.
   o Yes, most of the time
   o Yes, some of the time
   o Not very often
   o No, never

4. I have been anxious or worried for no good reason.
   o No, not at all
   o Hardly ever
   o Yes, some of the time
   o Yes, very often

5. I have felt scared or panicky for no very good reason.
   o Yes, quite a bit
   o Yes, sometimes
   o No, not much
   o No, not at all

6. Things have been getting on top of me.
   o Yes, most of the time I haven't been able to cope at all
   o Yes, sometimes I haven't been able to cope as usual
   o No, most of the time I have coped quite well
   o No, I have been coping as well as ever

7. I have been so unhappy that I have had difficulty sleeping.
   o Yes, most of the time
   o Yes, sometimes
   o Not very often
   o No, not at all

8. I have felt sad or miserable.
o   Yes, most of the time
o   Yes, quit often
o   No, not very often
o   No, not at all

9. I have been so unhappy that I have been crying.
o   Yes, most of the time
o   Yes, quite often
o   Only occasionally
o   No, never

10. The thought of harming myself has occurred to me.
o   Yes, quite often
o   Sometimes
o   Hardly ever
o   Never

Scoring:

For questions 1, 2, and 4, these are scored as 0, 1, 2, or 3, with the top box scored as 3. For questions 3 and 5 to 10, they are scored reversed, with the top box scored as 3 and the bottom box scored as 0.

The maximum score is thirty possible points. There is an indication of possible depression with a score of ten or greater. Pay special attention to question 10 as it relates to suicidal ideation.

Women who score greater than 10 on the scale are referred to a mental health specialist to see if she has postpartum depression and for treatment, if indicated.

The Beck Depression Inventory

Some obstetricians and psychiatrists prefer the Beck Depression Inventory, which is a general screening tool for the detection of depression. It is a twenty-one-point questionnaire that is self-taken and self-scored. The Beck Depression Inventory goes as follows:

1.
0   I do not feel sad
1   I feel sad
2   I am sad all the time, and I can't snap out of it
3   I am so sad and unhappy that I can't stand it

2.

0   I am not particularly discouraged about the future
1   I feel discouraged about the future
2   I feel I have nothing to look forward to
3   I feel the future is hopeless and that things cannot improve

3.

0   I do not feel like a failure
1   I feel I have failed more than the average person
2   As I look back on my life, all I can see is a lot of failures
3   I am a complete failure as a person

4.

0   I get as much satisfaction out of things as I used to
1   I don't enjoy things the way I used to
2   I don't get real satisfaction out of anything anymore
3   I am dissatisfied or bored with everything.

5.

0   I don't feel particularly guilty
1   I feel guilty a good part of the time
2   I feel quite guilty most of the time
3   I feel guilty all of the time

6.

0   I don't feel I am being punished
1   I feel I may be punished
2   I expect to be punished
3   I feel I am being punished

7.

0   I don't feel disappointed in myself
1   I am disappointed in myself
2   I am disgusted with myself
3   I hate myself

8.

0   I don't feel I am any worse than anybody else
1   I am critical of myself for my weaknesses or mistakes
2   I blame myself all the time for my faults
3   I blame myself for everything bad that happens

9.

0   I don't have any thoughts of killing myself
1   I have thoughts of killing myself but would not carry them out
2   I would like to kill myself
3   I would kill myself if I had the chance

10.

0   I don't cry any more than usual
1   I cry more now than I used to
2   I cry all the time now
3   I used to be able to cry, but now I can't cry even though I want to

11.

0   I am no more irritated by things than I ever was
1   I am slightly more irritated now than usual
2   I am quite annoyed or irritated a good deal of the time
3   I feel irritated all of the time

12.

0   I have not lost interest in other people
1   I am less interested in other people than I used to be
2   I have lost most of my interest in other people
3   I have lost all of my interest in other people

13.

0   I make decisions as well as I ever could
1   I put off making decisions more than I used to
2   I have greater difficulty in making decisions more than I used to
3   I can't make decisions at all anymore

14.

0   I don't feel that I look any worse than I used to
1   I am worried that I am looking old or unattractive
2   I feel there are permanent changes in my appearance that make me look
    unattractive
3   I believe that I look ugly

15.

0   I can work as well as before
1   It takes an extra effort to get started at doing something
2   I have to push myself very hard to do anything

3   I can't do any work at all

16.
0   I can sleep as well as usual
1   I don't sleep as well as I used to
2   I wake up several hours earlier than I used to and find it hard to get back to sleep
3   I wake up several hours earlier than I used to and cannot get back to sleep

17.
0   I don't get more tired than usual
1   I get tired more easily than I used to
2   I get tired from doing almost anything
3   I am too tired to do anything

18.
0   My appetite is no worse than usual
1   My appetite is not as good as it used to be
2   My appetite is much worse now
3   I have no appetite at all anymore

19.
0   I haven't lost much weight, if any, lately
1   I have lost more than 5 pounds
2   I have lost more than 10 pounds
3   I have lost more than 15 pounds

20.
0   I am no worried about my health than usual
1   I am worried about physical problems like aches, pains, or upset stomach
2   I am very worried about physical problems, and it is hard to think of much else
3   I am so worried about my physical problems that I cannot think of anything else

21.
0   I have not noticed any recent change in my interest in sex
1   I am less interested in sex than I used to be
2   I have almost no interest in sex
3   I have lost interest in sex completely

Interpreting the Beck Depression Inventory

Now that you have completed the questionnaire, add up the score for each of the twenty-one questions by counting the number to the right of each question you marked. The highest possible total for the whole test would be sixty-three. This would mean that you circled 3 on all twenty-one questions. Since the lowest possible score for each question is zero, the lowest possible score would be zero. This would mean you circled 0 on each question. You can evaluate your depression according to the table below:

Total Score: _____

Levels of Depression: 1–10 These ups and downs are considered normal
11–16 Mild mood disturbance
17–20 Borderline clinical depression
21–30 Moderate depression
31–40 Severe depression
Over 40 indicates extreme depression

If you have a consistent score of seventeen or more, you may need some medical or psychiatric depression.

Of the two tests, the Edinburgh Postnatal Depression Score is considered the preferable test for women at risk for postnatal depression and can be given over the phone or in person to the postpartum mother. The Beck Depression Inventory includes sleep and appetite questions as well as weight changes that are a natural part of childbirth and therefore does not give a complete picture.

Babies born in Cleveland, Ohio, have a slimmer chance of celebrating their first birthdays than those born in almost any other major US city. Black babies born here are as likely to survive their first year as babies born in Syria or Jordan. They're more than two times as likely to die as babies born to white mothers. White infants in our city don't do a lot better when you compare their odds of survival against kids born in the rest of Ohio, the nation, or other developed countries. They're as likely to survive to a first birthday as kids born in Cyprus or Ukraine.

—*Brie Zeltner,* The Plain Dealer, *12-10-15*

Chapter 13

INFANT MORTALITY IN THE UNITED STATES

Infant mortality is important as it indicates the health and well-being of a nation. Although infant mortality in the United States has declined significantly since 1933, it is still much higher than the infant mortality rate in many other developed countries. In 1988, the United States ranked twenty-third in world rankings for infant mortality rate from twelfth place in 1960 (1).

This unfavorable standing of the United States in rankings of infant mortality rate stems in a large part from the racial disparity in infant survival rates and in the socioeconomic differences that have existed in the country for a long time (2). There are considerable differences in infant mortality among Caucasians, blacks, and other ethnic groups in the United States. There are also variables to consider, such as family income and education between the races and ethnic groups.

A thorough analysis of the prior trends, current status, and future course of mortality among infants is important not only for developing adequate maternal and child health programs but also for formulating the overall health plan in the United States. Unfortunately, no systematic effort has yet been made to bring together a discussion of longstanding trends in infant mortality rate and implications for the future.

Data on infant mortality rate can be obtained by accessing the National Vital Statistics System, which provides information from 1950 to 1991, as well as the National Linked Birth and Infant Death Data Sets and the 1988 National Maternal and Infant Health Survey. Differences in income among families with infant deaths cannot, however, be directly examined through the National Vital Statistics System or through linked birth and infant death files. Live birth statistics can be used to make up the difference.

The average decline in infant mortality rate during the period of 1950 through 1991 was quite significant with an average decline of more than 3 percent per year. At times, the infant mortality rate was less than that (between 1950 and 1965), with a decline of only 1 percent per year. The infant mortality rate declined more significantly from 1966 to 1981 with a reduction of 50 percent during that period.

Trends in infant mortality by ethnicity were somewhat different between 1950 and 1991. The infant mortality rate for Caucasian infants was 3.23 percent per year, while the rate for African American infants dropped by 2.89 percent per year. There were times in which the rate of infant death was about the same between the races, but this was not the norm. In 1950, there were 43.9 infant deaths per 1,000 live births among African Americans, which was 64 percent higher than the rate for Caucasian infants. By 1991, the infant mortality rate among African Americans had deteriorated, with the rate of infant death being 2.2 times the infant mortality rate among Caucasians.

When referring to neonatal mortality, we are referring to any infant death that occurs during the first twenty-seven days of life, while postneonatal mortality refers to infant deaths between twenty-eight days and one year of life. The causes of death are differentiated according to perinatal conditions, congenital anomalies, SIDS, and other causes of death. In the years 1985–1987, for example, the total number of Caucasian babies who died in the neonatal period was 5.5 per 1,000 live births, while the number of African American babies who died in the neonatal period was 12.0 per 1,000 live births.

Between the years 1950 and 1991, the rate of death in the neonatal period declined much faster than the postneonatal death rate for the total population. The average percentage decreases per year for neonatal mortality was 3.41, while the postneonatal mortality rate declined only 2.46 percent.

The trends in neonatal and postnatal death rates by race show some interesting patterns. The neonatal mortality rate declined at a considerably quicker rate than the postnatal mortality rate for Caucasian infants. The average percentage decreases per year were 3.65 for the neonatal death rate and 2.27 for the postneonatal death rate.

For the African American infants, however, the opposite was true. The postneonatal mortality rate during 1950–1991 declined more rapidly than their neonatal death rate, with the average percentage decreases being 3.09 percent for neonatal death rate and 2.78 percent for the postneonatal death rate. As in infant death rate, the neonatal death rate has seen an increasing racial inequality over time, with African American infants having a 43 percent greater risk of dying compared with Caucasian infants in the neonatal period in 1950. The same figure for 1991 showed a 130 percent increase in a black infant dying over a white infant.

Postneonatal mortality has, on the other hand, narrowed between Caucasians and African Americans, especially in the early years. For example, in 1960, an

African American infant was 2.9 times more likely to die than Caucasian infants in this period, while in 1991, the relative rates of mortality in the postneonatal period was only 2.1 times that of Caucasian infants.

Significant differences in neonatal mortality and postneonatal mortality can also be found among other racial and ethnic groups, such as American Indians, Chinese, Filipinos, Japanese, Hawaiians, Mexicans, and other Hispanic groups. The highest neonatal mortality rate was found among Puerto Ricans, with a neonatal mortality rate of 7.3 infants per 1,000 live births and a postneonatal mortality rate of 3.7 per 1,000 live births.

On the other hand, the infant mortality rate (the total of neonatal and postneonatal mortality rates) was considerably lower for Japanese and Chinese infants than for any other group. When compared with Caucasian infants, Chinese and Japanese infants had a 30 percent and 23 percent lower infant mortality rate, respectively.

There is a difference in infant mortality rate when comparing their parents' educational levels. The US infant mortality rate for Caucasians reaching the twelfth grade level was 18 deaths per 1,000 live births between 1964 and 1967, while the same figure for African Americans was 34.5 infant deaths per 1,000 live births per year. The differences leveled off as the education level rose past the twelfth grade. The effect of maternal education on infant mortality rate appeared to be more significant for Caucasians compared with African American infants. Infant death rates among African Americans was significantly higher at all levels of education.

Between 1964 and 1987, the infant mortality rate fell considerably across all educational backgrounds for both Caucasians and African Americans, although infants who had mothers with sixteen or more years of education had the greatest percentage decline in mortality rates. The infants who benefited the least from their mothers' education were those born to mothers who had nine to eleven years of education.

Like educational background, family income in general was inversely proportional to infant mortality rate. In 1988, for example, the infant mortality rate among Caucasians who were born to families with an income of less than $10,000 per year was 11.2 per 1,000 live births, while the infant mortality rate among African American infants born to families with an income of less than $10,000 per year was 19.3 per 1,000 live births.

Again, in 1988, the infant mortality rate among those infants born to families with an income of $10,000 or less was almost twice as big as the infant mortality rate among infants born to families who made $35,000 or more (11.2 compared with 7.2 among Caucasians and 19.3 compared with 16.6 among African Americans). Note that even when income is taken into account, the infant mortality rate was much higher in African Americans compared with Caucasians at all income levels.

Causes of Infant Mortality

The ten leading causes of infant death in 1991 include the following:

1. Congenital anomalies
2. Sudden infant death syndrome
3. Short duration of gestation
4. Respiratory distress syndrome
5. Complications of pregnancy
6. Complications of cord or placenta
7. Accidents and adverse effects
8. Infections
9. Pneumonia and influenza
10. Birth asphyxia

The second, third, and fourth leading causes of death for the total population were SIDS, prematurity, and respiratory distress syndrome at 14.5 percent, 11.3 percent, and 7 percent of all infant deaths during that year.

There were differences in the leading cause of death among Caucasian infants and African American infants. For example, congenital anomalies were the leading cause of death among Caucasian infants, while they were the third leading cause of death among African American infants. Prematurity and low birthweight made up the third leading cause of death among Caucasian infants, while they were the leading cause of death among African American infants. Prematurity and low birth weight accounted for one in every six deaths among African American infants.

When comparing infant causes of death between 1981 and 1991, the greatest decline in mortality occurred for intrauterine hypoxia and birth asphyxia, respiratory distress syndrome, and pneumonia and influenza. These declines were found in all ethnic groups. There was, however, a disconcerting trend in infant death rate among African American infants who died from prematurity at a greater rate in 1991 compared with in 1981 by a factor of 9 percent.

Race and ethnic differences in infant mortality by cause of death were higher among African Americans compared with Caucasians for each of the ten leading causes of death in both 1981 and 1991. The ratios, however, increased in deaths due to prematurity and low birth weight, pneumonia and influenza, and perinatal infections between Caucasians and African Americans, worsening the already large racial disparity in mortality from these causes of infant death.

Of all the groups, American Indian infants were at the greatest risk of dying from SIDS with a mortality risk that was 2.7 times greater than among Caucasian babies. The risk of dying from SID was about twice that among African Americans compared with Caucasians.

Conclusions about Infant Mortality

Over the past four decades, there has been a dramatic decrease in infant mortality rate largely because of decreases in death from things like pneumonia and influenza, respiratory distress syndrome, prematurity and low birth weight. Despite these reductions, however, there is still a large disparity in infant mortality between Caucasian babies and African American babies. In fact, the disparity has increased over time that the risk of infant death is currently more than twice that in African Americans compared with that in Caucasians. Significant differences in infant mortality rate exist by education and overall family income.

Despite remarkable successes in improving maternal and child health over the last four decades, the United States has not made enough progress in meeting several health objectives in this population. The infant mortality rate in the United States remains higher than in most other developed countries perhaps because of the excess mortality rates observed among certain minority groups and among those in low socioeconomic status groups. There remains room for substantial improvement in infant mortality rate in the United States.

I was on a roller coaster ride for the
first two weeks.
I was happy... I was sad.
Happy... crying.
Happy... tired.
Happy... overwhelmed.
Happy... exhausted.
I didn't know how I felt.

Chapter 14

BABY BLUES

Many women experience hormonal and psychological changes that don't completely fit the criteria for postpartum depression and are instead said to have the "baby blues." The onset of this condition is between the first two to three weeks of the baby's life and is known to occur in up to 50–80 percent of pregnancies. Unlike postpartum depression, the baby blues go away with support and time, although they are considered a risk factor for postpartum depression, with 25 percent of women going on to develop postpartum depression (82).

The common symptoms of baby blues include frequent episodes of crying and tearfulness, excessive fatigue, anxiety, and mood swings. As mentioned, the baby blues often pass without any intervention or with good social and emotional support on the part of the woman's family and social system. The major difference between baby blues and postpartum depression is the short time frame involved in having baby blues. Baby blues also do not interfere with the mother's interpersonal relationship with the child and her functioning.

"Nothing at all went as planned for my delivery...
My birth plan went out the window...
I thought I was going to die..."

Chapter 15

ACUTE STRESS DISORDER

Women can develop acute stress disorder (ASD) from the stresses of undergoing childbirth. The symptoms of acute stress disorder usually occur shortly after the birth of the infant and occur in about 1.5–6 percent of pregnancies.

Women at risk for acute stress disorder after childbirth are those who have suffered from some kind of birth trauma or adverse outcome in the birth process. Many have also suffered from some sort of recent trauma or a history of trauma (including child abuse and past sexual abuse). The symptoms can last for weeks after the delivery if left untreated. In order to qualify for acute stress disorder, the symptoms must last at least three days, although they can persist for months. Women with ASD often have symptoms similar to those seen in posttraumatic stress disorder (PTSD).

Acute stress disorder is exacerbated in the postpartum state under the following circumstances:

- A traumatic birth
- An extremely painful birth
- An adverse birth outcome
- The threat of death to the mother or infant
- A threat to the physical integrity of the mother or infant

Symptoms of Acute Stress Disorder

In order to qualify for the diagnosis of acute stress disorder, the woman needs to have at least three of the following dissociative symptoms:

- Having a reduced awareness of one's surroundings
- Feeling numb, detached, or emotionally unresponsive, especially when it comes to the infant
- Derealization, in which the environment seems unreal or strange
- Depersonalization, in which the thoughts or emotions the woman has don't seem like they belong to her or the thoughts or emotions don't seem real.
- The woman develops dissociative amnesia, in which she cannot remember the birth or other parts of what she perceives as a traumatic event

The woman will often reexperience the traumatic event in the hours to days following the delivery. She may have recurring thoughts, images, flashbacks, or illusions of the traumatic event. She may feel as if she is reliving the labor and delivery. She may suffer from extreme distress when reminded of the labor and delivery.

Avoidance is one of the main symptoms of acute stress disorder. The woman may avoid stimuli that results in remembering or reexperiencing the labor and delivery. She may be disturbed by the nurses and doctors involved in the delivery, by her infant, by conversations around the birth process, by the hospital, and by anything that reminds her of her trauma.

A woman with ASD will be anxious and will have increased arousal. This can manifest itself as having the following symptoms:

- Difficulty sleeping
- Feelings of irritability
- Difficulty concentrating
- Being unable to sit still or stop moving
- Being tense around the baby or always on guard
- Being easily startled when the infant cries or when suddenly approached

The distress a woman feels when she has ASD can disrupt the maternal-infant bond and can disrupt her social interactions. She may start a task and be unable to complete it. She may keep her symptoms a secret and be unable to tell her doctor, her family, or the hospital staff about her distress.

Diagnosis of Acute Stress Disorder

A primary health care provider or a mental health provider may diagnose acute stress disorder by asking the woman questions about the delivery and the symptoms she is experiencing. Other disorders need to be ruled out, including the following:

- Side effects of medication
- Drug abuse in the mother
- Health conditions contributing to anxiety
- Other psychiatric problems unrelated to the acute stressor

The doctor will take note of the symptoms to see if they qualify as acute stress disorder according to the Diagnostic and Statistical Manual of Psychiatric Disorders.

Treatment of Acute Distress Disorder

If the health care provider feels that the symptoms are suggestive of acute stress disorder, a number of treatments may be suggested. These include the following:

- A psychiatric consult to see if you need medications or a psychiatric admission
- Hospitalization if there is a risk of suicide or harm to the fetus
- Social services assistance if care is to be continued as an outpatient
- Psychiatric education so the woman better understands her disorder
- Antianxiety medications, selective serotonin reuptake inhibitors (SSRIs), and other types of antidepressants
- Psychotherapy, in particular cognitive behavioral therapy, which may help prevent the onset of PTSD arising out of ASD
- Exposure-based therapies
- Hypnotherapy

Outlook of Acute Stress Disorder

Untreated acute stress disorder often leads to posttraumatic stress disorder. The diagnosis of PTSD is made if the anxiety and related symptoms last for more than one month and result in an excess of stress and poor functioning. Treatment of ASD may minimize the chances of having PTSD. About half of all cases of PTSD can be relieved within six months with proper treatment, although some people will have symptoms lasting for many years, interfering with subsequent pregnancies and deliveries.

Prevention of Acute Stress Disorder

There is no clear way to prevent acute stress disorder because every woman's experience in labor and delivery is different. Good patient education about the process of labor and delivery and good pain control during labor can help reduce the risk of ASD following the delivery (62, 63).

"On Monday I went to my OB/GYN
and told him what was going on...
He had me go and talk to a counselor on Tuesday...
Who told me to go to the psychiatrist on Wed. Nothing happened.
Then I took the baby to the pediatrician on Thursday,
and he is the only one who really helped me..."

"I thought I was going crazy...
Until my doctor told me that this had a name...
And that there was excellent treatment...
And that I would feel much better soon...
and recover..."

Chapter 16

POSTPARTUM DEPRESSION

Postpartum depression has a strong effect on the infant-caregiver relationship. This relationship is designed to be a special unit that is associated with a complex set of interactions, including social and ecological factors that together shape the development of the infant. Infants need a quality bond with their mother in order to shape their attachment security. A good maternal-infant bond starts the process of cognitive, socioemotional, moral, and self-regulation in the infant. It helps shape a child's trajectory into later childhood and adolescence. The infant needs a great deal of maternal attunement in the early months of their existence in order to develop self-regulation and a positive self-image.

Postpartum depression impacts maternal-infant attachment and maternal attunement to the child. In general, postpartum depression is characterized as a nonpsychotic depressive disorder that is similar to depression at other times in a woman's life. The onset of postpartum depression can happen any time after the birth of a child, but it usually occurs four to six weeks after the birth of the child but can occur at any time within the first year of the child's life (64). An estimated 10–20 percent of women suffer from postpartum depression. It has been found to occur at a much higher rate among low-income populations (with a rate of between 23 and 52 percent) (65).

Symptoms of Postpartum Depression

In some cases, the baby blues escalate to postpartum depression. In such cases, the woman can develop the following symptoms:

• Depressed mood
• Extreme sadness

- Crying spells
- Insecurity, particularly around caring for the newborn
- Anxiety, usually related to parenting
- Sleep disturbances
- Changes in appetite
- Poor concentration
- Episodes of confusion
- Increased irritability
- A sense of loss of self
- A sense of isolation
- A feeling of worthlessness
- Sensations of shame
- Feelings of guilt, particularly around parenting
- Increased anger
- Having an inability to care for herself and her family

I do not feel loving toward my baby and can't even go through the motions to take care of him/her.

—*mother with postpartum depression*

In severe cases, the postpartum depression can further escalate to postpartum psychosis, which will be discussed in a later chapter.

Risks for Postpartum Depression

Women at the highest risk for postpartum depression are women who have suffered from depression prior to the pregnancy or depression during the pregnancy. Women who have had postpartum depression in prior pregnancies are also at a greater risk. In fact, women who have had a prior history of postpartum depression run the risk of getting it again at a rate of about 25 percent (66).

There are several other factors that contribute to a mother getting postpartum depression. These include infant factors, maternal factors, and ecological factors.

There is an increased risk of developing postpartum depression in women who have suffered from high-risk pregnancies, infants with poor motor functioning, low-birth-weight infants, prematurity, and newborn irritability. If the mother has had depression during the pregnancy, this has been found to increase maternal cortisol levels. Cortisol crosses the placental barrier and causes stress-related physiological dysregulation in the infant, who also has higher cortisol levels. The infant's inability to self-regulate their own physiological rhythms cause a disruption in the maternal-child synchrony (70).

There are maternal factors that play into a woman developing postpartum depression. Any woman with a history of major depression can suffer from a relapse during or after the pregnancy. This risk goes up when she stops taking her antidepressant therapy during the pregnancy. This causes an increased risk of relapse both during and after the pregnancy is over with. The mother's attitude toward being pregnant and having a baby has an impact on her overall mood and is predictive of postpartum depression. The presence of a supportive father can be protective against postpartum depression. If the father has a positive feeling about the pregnancy, there is a decreased level of postpartum depression and a greater degree of maternal attachment to her baby (71).

There are psychological factors in the mother that predispose her to developing postpartum depression. These include the following:

- There are normal psychological changes associated with having a child that affect all women but affect some women more than others.
- Having an unplanned pregnancy with ambivalence over having a child
- Having unrealistic expectations of motherhood
- Being a "perfectionist" prior to the pregnancy
- Being a first time mother, which is often associated with a significant lifestyle change
- Having unresolved losses, such as a prior miscarriage, abortion, infertility, or postpartum tubal ligation
- Having a recent stressor, such as financial difficulties, a recent move, divorce, job change, or illness
- Having negative childhood experiences, such as a history of child abuse, neglect, or posttraumatic stress disorder
- Having a poor-quality relationship with the baby's father
- Having a poor support system
- Being a single mother
- Having a poor-quality relationship with the baby or infant who is ill, has colic, or spent time in the NICU
- Having a poor relationship with the other children

The biological maternal factors that play into getting postpartum depression include the following:

- The normal hormonal changes associated with having a baby
- Changes in brain chemicals after delivery
- Becoming hypothyroid in the postpartum state (This happens at a rate of about 5–10 percent during the first year after delivery of an infant.)
- Having multiple births

- Having a history of infertility
- Having a history of sexual abuse
- Having a history of premenstrual dysphoric disorder (PMDD)
- Having a past history of mental illness, which increases the risk by a factor of 3 to 4
- Having a history of postpartum depression (The recurrence rate is 50–70 percent.)
- Having a complicated pregnancy or delivery
- Suffering from sleep deprivation
- Being socially isolate
- Having major life events or stressors in the pregnancy or postpartum state

There are also several ecological factors that play into the development of postpartum depression. There is an increased risk if the mother experiences a high degree of stress, greater numbers of life events, low family income, and decreased social support. Support around child-rearing, including closeness to mothers who have children the same age as her own, is associated with a decreased risk of postpartum depression. Mothers who work show an increase in their interest in their infants, while nonworking mothers have a higher rate of negative facial expressions toward their infant as well as irritation and disinterest in their infants (72).

Other risk factors impacting child development include having a history of mental illness in the mother, a history of anxiety, rigid parental beliefs, and unusual attitudes regarding child development. Things like having the head of the household in an unskilled occupation, lower educational status in the mother, being of a racial or ethnic minority, low degree of family support, a higher number of stressful life events, and a larger family size also increase the risk of postpartum depression. The more risk factors the mother has, the higher is the probability of poor academic achievement, lower intellectual function, and poor social outcomes. Single mothers are often poorer than married mothers, and this makes the outcome in the child much worse.

Delving into Postpartum Depression

Besides the abovementioned symptoms, women with postpartum depression often have reduced eye contact with others, a slow rate of speech, and a decrease in emotional responsiveness and expressiveness. Women with postpartum depression tend to be slow to respond to infant cries and infant distress. They vocalize less often with their children, look less at their children, and are less involved in infant synchrony, rhythmic imitation, and joint activity with their child.

These are mothers who talk less about the activities and abilities of their infants and have touch that is more functional and less affectionate toward their child. The interactions between mother and baby is further impaired the longer the depression lasts, and they display less face-to-face interaction with their baby. They are less competent in feeding the child in the postpartum period (67).

Women with postpartum depression are often extremely preoccupied. This promotes an insecure attachment in the infants and as they grow to become toddlers and preschoolers. When the mother responds by being unpredictable, unavailable, rejecting, or insensitive, the child will learn not to seek out the mother whenever distressed and will behave in an ambivalent manner toward her. As infants, they learn to see the world and the people in it as potentially rejecting and untrustworthy; they soon see themselves as unworthy of love (68).

When the mother suffers from maternal depression, the children have a wide range of difficulties not limited to lower frustration tolerance, high rates of noncompliant behavior, emotional dysregulation, emotional liability, diminished positive affect, and inability to soothe themselves. There is EEG evidence to suggest that these children suffer from increased negative affectivity and decreased ability to regulate their own arousal, and they tend to cry more (69).

These children also have problems regulating attention and emotion, which impacts their overall perceptual learning. Decreased rates of infant-directed speech by depressed mothers is directly related to poor performance on tests of cognitive function, even as early as two months of age. The infant also suffers from poor health because their depressed mothers are less likely to nurse their infants and less likely to be compliant with immunizations and well-infant visits.

Maybe I should have never become a mother, I
think I may have made a mistake.

—*New mom*

Effects of PPD on the Infant and Child

A mother with postpartum depression has an influence on her developing child. Some of these influences result in the following:

- Language delays in the child
- Poor or insecure mother-infant attachment

- Behavioral problems in the child
- Lower cognitive performance in the child
- Mental health issues in the child
- Attention difficulties
- Having a withdrawn child that is often fussy, crying, or having temper tantrums
- Sleeping problems in the child
- Feeding or eating difficulties

As mentioned, there is reasonable evidence that maternal psychiatric disorders have a negative effect on child development. The child may be directly exposed to the psychiatric disorder of the mother, leading to the development of their own psychiatric or developmental disorder. There may also be an indirect impact related to the way the parent raises the child. Being a child in an environment where psychiatric problems are prevalent can impact the child. Genetic factors may also play a role (73).

The mother's state of mind affects the infant to a greater degree because the infant has an extreme amount of dependency on her, and she is likely to be the sole caretaker of the child. It is only natural that she wields a great deal of influence over the growth and development of the growing child.

There have been a number of studies examining the development of one- to two-year-old children whose mothers have suffered from postpartum depression (74). These studies have identified an association between maternal depression in the first year of the child's life and cognitive outcome of the child aged twelve to eighteen months. These infants had clear evidence of poor mental and motor development when compared with controls. This has held up in other studies. The boys of mothers with postpartum depression seemed to be particularly affected.

Compared with controls, infants of depressed mothers at eighteen months showed less interactive behavior with others, less sociability to strangers, less concentration, and an increased rate of negative responses. There was also an association between maternal depression and the development of insecure attachment in this age group. The most prominent type of attachment was of the avoidant type (75).

Studies have been done on behavioral problems as well. Researchers interviewed mothers with children who were eighteen months old using a modified version of a behavioral screening questionnaire and found that those mothers with depression were more likely to report behavioral problems in their child. The most common findings were disturbances in eating and sleeping, separation difficulties, and an increase in temper tantrums. Together, these findings indicate an elevated level of emotional disturbance in the time between one and two years of age among children whose mothers had postpartum depression.

The cognitive delays and level of attachment to the mother were more prominent among children raised by mothers with severe postpartum depression as opposed to mild maternal depression. It was also found to be more common when the mother was chronically depressed as opposed to intermittently depressed (76). The findings were still present even if the mother had already recovered at the time the infant was assessed. Another study found that the behavior problems, insecure attachment, and poor cognitive outcome in eighteen-month-old infants persisted even after the mother's postpartum depression had been resolved by six to eight months postpartum.

Parenting difficulties have also been found to be linked to abnormal development in the child. Even in women who had depression that had remitted, there was an increase in irritability in the mother and withdrawn behavior around their close family members. It could be that postpartum depression sets a pattern of relating to the child that remains compromised even when the depression has been resolved (77). It means that the maternal-child interactive style arising out of depression plays a greater role in infant development rather than the child's exposure to the actual depressive symptoms.

Children with disengaged mothers had a higher chance of having protest behavior, while children with mothers who were more intrusive had a higher chance of avoidant attachment (78). This has been confirmed in other studies.

Another possible cause of cognitive and behavioral deficits in children whose mothers suffered from postpartum depression is environmental adversity. Postpartum depression is often present in situations of personal and social diversity (79). This means that the association of postpartum depression and poor child outcome is as much related to overcrowding, marital discord, and poverty as it is to the depression itself.

One study (80) revealed that, among a group of women with postpartum depression, deficits in play with child and feeding were highly linked to the presence of adversity in the child. Nondepressed women, who also had significant environmental adversity, also showed similar deficits in interaction with their children when compared with depressed women.

Certain infant characteristics such as poor motor control and irritability, which were measured prior to the onset of postpartum depression (at ten days postpartum), increased the risk of depression in the mother at a later time.

In conclusion, it is clear that postpartum depression in the mother carries a risk to the mother-infant relationship and the resultant developmental outcome. The adverse effects of postpartum depression in the mother appear to be related to maternal mood and parenting style. The impact is more severe when the depression is prolonged and severe and when it happens in the context of family and social adversity.

My sister should've been her mother not me. I think of killing myself, 'cause I just can't do this... The system will take care of her. She's a better mother than I am. I'm no good. I scream at the baby because she cries, I just can't take it anymore.

Single mom living with her sister, lost her job during the pregnancy, drinking after the baby is asleep.

Diagnosing Postpartum Depression

Clearly, all postpartum women need to be screened for postpartum depressive symptoms. This can be done through a structured interview that incorporates the following questions:

- "How are things at home?"
- "Are you sleeping okay when the baby sleeps? How long does it take to go to sleep after the baby is asleep? How long do you sleep?"
- "Are there any changes in your appetite?
- "Are you experiencing any anxiety?"
- "Are you afraid to be alone with the baby?"
- "Are you afraid you might lose control?"
- "Do you feel more irritable or angry than usual?"
- "Are you worried about the way you feel right now?"
- "Are you afraid you might lose control?"
- "Are you worried about the way you feel right now?"
- "Are you afraid of any thoughts you are having?"
- "Does your partner know how you are feeling?"
- "Have you ever had thoughts of hurting yourself or the baby?"
- "Is there anything you are afraid to tell me but think I should know?"

When this interview is completed, there may be red flags—things the woman says that raises the index of suspicion that she might be suffering from postpartum depression. These include some of the following:

- "I have not slept at all in forty-eight hours or more."
- "I have lost a lot weight without trying to."

- "I do not feel loving toward my baby."
- "I can't even go through the motions to take care of my baby."
- "I feel like such a bad mother."
- "I'm afraid I might harm myself in order to escape the pain."
- "I am afraid I might actually do something to hurt the baby."
- "I hear sounds or voices when no one is around."
- "I feel that my thoughts are not my own or that they are totally out of my control."
- "Maybe I should have never become a mother; I think I may have made a mistake."

If any of these or similar statements are made by the new mother, these are red flags and indicate she needs an immediate referral for further psychiatric evaluation and management.

Tips for the Professional

When dealing with a postpartum mother, it is important to take these tips into account:

- Do not assume that if she looks good, she is fine.
- Do not assume this will get better on its own.
- Encourage her to get a comprehensive evaluation if you are concerned with her statements or behavior.
- Take her concerns seriously.
- Let her know when you are available if she needs you.
- Inform her of support resources for postpartum depression.

Prognosis for Postpartum Depression

The prognosis for postpartum depression is excellent if treated adequately, although these women are at an increased risk for major depression in the future (unrelated to pregnancy). The children of mothers who have suffered from postpartum depression are at risk for behavioral and cognitive deficits even if the postpartum depression has been treated.

In high-risk women, it is important to step up the nursing intervention by having increased visits to new moms by a nurse who understands postpartum depression and can recognize its early signs during their home visits. The sooner the woman is treated for her depression, the sooner she recovers and the less impact this has on the developing child (81).

"I finally told my husband that he and my daughter would be better off without me—that I was not a good mother or wife. I felt like things were never going to get better—that I would never feel happy again."

Post partum mom

Chapter 17

TREATMENT OF POSTPARTUM DEPRESSION

Normally, depression is treated with antidepressant medication. Unfortunately, many women are not willing to take antidepressants during pregnancy and while breast-feeding because the medications used to treat depression cross the placental barrier and can be found in breast milk. The truth is, however, no difference has been found in the treatment of postpartum depression when psychotherapy was used alone versus when it is used along with antidepressants (82).

There have been many studies showing that psychotherapy alone can reduce maternal symptoms of postpartum depression. The main approaches in psychotherapy used for depression include nondirective counseling, cognitive behavioral therapy, and psychodynamics. Antidepressants are used when psychotherapy does not work on its own or when the mother has moderate to severe postpartum depression. In order to use medications, the doctor must inform her of the benefits of taking the medication versus the risk of not taking antidepressants to treat the depression.

Just treating the symptoms of postpartum depression is generally not helpful and will not improve the maternal-infant bond or protect the child from the negative consequences of having a mother with postpartum depression (83). It can lessen the stress in the mother around issues of parenting and improves the mother's rating of the emotional and behavioral condition of the child; however, real changes in the maternal-infant interaction and the outcome of the child have not been reported. Children born to mothers who have suffered from postpartum depression still have issues around attachment security, more episodes of negative affect, decreased cognitive development, and an increase in internalizing problems.

Tackling the Maternal-Fetal Relationship

Any therapy directed at the treatment of postpartum depression must include the infant in the treatment in an attempt to restore the disruptions that have occurred in the maternal-infant relationship. This is called mother-infant psychodynamic psychotherapy or PPT. In this type of therapy, the mother is taught how to understand the influence of her previous relationships on her current interactions with her baby. Therapy, in this situation, helps link the mother's current parenting concerns with her own past experience in childhood. This insight helps promote greater competency in the mother's ability to interact with her child (83).

Psychodynamic psychotherapy can help a mother by teaching her the basics of attachment theory and providing her with guidance that is focused on improving her responsiveness to the infant and her sensitivity toward the infant's needs and decreases her level of intrusiveness surrounding the baby. The mother's postpartum depression improves, and she gains competence in her role as a parent (84).

With this type of therapy, the infants develop better cognitive functioning and an improvement in emotional regulation. There is a greater shift in the infant developing a secure attachment to their mother. The therapy also helps mothers who later suffer a relapse in their depression so that the child can maintain a high level of cognitive functioning.

Psychodynamic psychotherapy not only lessens the degree of postpartum depression but also improves the cognitive functioning in the infant when measured six months later (84).

Doing maternal-infant psychotherapy in a group setting has also been used to treat postpartum depression (84). The groups make use of a focused mother-baby group as well as a group dedicated to infant development and a group just for the mothers. The group dynamics reinforce the mother's relationship with the infant and allow them to see their children in a different way. Mothers develop a better positive affect and better communication skills with their babies.

Helping the Mother in the Home

Seeing the mother and her infant in the home environment has been found to be just as effective as mother-baby psychotherapy. They work with the mother as an individual in her own surroundings and also consider the relationship between the depressed mother and her infant. This type of approach can also work with the ecological issues surrounding postpartum depression, such as poverty and poor marital relationships.

Programs based out of the home make use of public health resources and improve mother-baby interaction, decreasing the mother's social isolation while emphasizing her important role as the main source of emotional security for the infant. Things like infant massage can be taught to the mother. This can improve the child's internal regulation, improve the child's temperament, and increase the child's sociability. Increased serotonin levels are found in the infant as well as decreased stress hormone levels, lessening the stress and probable depression in the infant as well (85).

Infant massage has been found to be particularly helpful. The depressed mother can gain increased sensitivity to her baby's cues, and there is an improvement in the interactions between mother and baby over time.

There are findings in the mother that suggest she is likely to have a more chronic course of postpartum depression. These include activation of the EEG in the right frontal lobe, increased cortisol levels, increased norepinephrine levels, increased serotonin levels, and a decrease in vagal tone and her positive interaction with her child (86).

In one study (86), women who were found to be at a higher risk for chronic depression received a more comprehensive intervention at home. Things like infant massage, music therapy, visual imagery, progressive relaxation, and coaching were provided in order to increase the mother's sensitivity to her baby and increase infant's responsiveness. Educational and skill development was provided for the mother. This resulted in an improved biochemical profile in the mother, along with lower levels of depression and better interactions with the child. The infant gained weight and scored higher on social functioning and cognitive function.

Treatment of postpartum depression is somewhat unique in that a specific life-changing event is coinciding with the onset of depression, namely, the transition from woman to mother. The at-risk population already has a steady contact with the health care system, making it easier to intervene if problems arise.

Unfortunately, while this disorder affects 10–15 percent of the general postnatal population and between 23 and 52 percent of women in a low-income status, more than 50 percent of cases go undetected (87).

According to the American Academy of Pediatrics, fiftyseven percent of pediatricians report feeling somewhat responsible for the recognition of postpartum depression (87). Unfortunately, seventy three percent of this same population report not having enough time to educate and counsel mothers. Seventy percent felt they had little time to obtain the mother's history, and sixty four percent felt they didn't have the training to diagnose the disorder or counsel mothers at risk. Forty-eight percent felt they didn't have the knowledge to provide mothers with treatment choices.

Infants are particularly susceptible to the damaging effects of postpartum depression in the first few weeks of life. This is the time when obstetricians, pediatrician, and midwives need to be especially aware of the symptoms of the disorder and begin a dialogue with the mother regarding any symptom she may be experiencing.

The best times to intervene and help these mothers is during these crucial periods:

- During prenatal visits prior to the birth of the baby
- In the early days while the mother is still in the hospital
- During scheduled visits after the baby is born

During Prenatal Visits

Prenatal visits provide an opportunity for the obstetrical staff to screen the mother for risk factors and for symptoms of antenatal depression, which carries a risk for postpartum depression. This type of screening costs little and should include the mother's own psychiatric history and that of her family. Environmental stressors and the mother's support system can be assessed at the same time.

The intervention can be discussed using a structured interview with the pregnant woman. There are questionnaires that may help the process, including the Edinburgh Postnatal Depression Scale (EPDS). This is a ten-item measurement for women about to give birth and for new mothers. It carries a strong predictive ability in detecting postpartum depression (88). Women found to be depressed in their pregnancy can begin to receive treatment even before the delivery of their infant. Considerations of antidepressant medications and referral to community support systems can help prevent the onset of postpartum depression. This early intervention can lead to a better prognosis.

While in the Hospital

The woman can be assessed for signs of depression before she leaves the hospital with her infant. Things like poor motor function, newborn irritability, and low birth weight can point toward mothers who are at the highest risk. Recognizing these things help provide an opportunity for intervention in high-risk mothers. Such mothers can receive intervention for psychotherapy and antidepressant medications before they take her baby home.

During Postnatal Visits

The onset of postpartum depression luckily coincides with time in which she is seen for a regularly scheduled postpartum visit. This provides yet another opportunity for mothers to be assessed for postpartum depression as they are already in contact with knowledgeable health care providers. The Edinburgh Postnatal Depression Scale can be given at that time and can identify mothers at a higher risk for depression. This is when a referral can be made to a mental health professional for further questioning and treatment if necessary. Women who need antidepressants can be given the option of taking them before the symptoms become fully ingrained, provided they know the risks and benefits of taking such medication.

Because the mother-baby relationship is strongly influenced by the environment in which they live including her family, culture, and community, this can be assessed during home visits to check on the health of both the mother and the infant. This may mean assessing the effect that other family members, the mother's culture, and the mother's community at the same time, providing educational and vocational help along with community-based support groups or educational groups.

There is no perfect decision, and no decision is risk free. Patients need to know about the risk of exposure to medications and they need to know about the risk of untreated disease.

—*Dr. Lee Cohen, University of Iowa,* Neuropsychiatry Reviews, *June 2001*

Treatment Using Antidepressants and Electroconvulsive Therapy

Most cases of postpartum depression can be managed on an outpatient basis; however, if infant safety or maternal suicidality becomes a concern, the mother needs to be hospitalized. We have discussed the impact of psychotherapy on postpartum depression as well as the possibility of using medications to treat cases of moderate to severe postpartum depression.

The use of medications and psychotherapy are considered first-line treatments for mothers who are not psychotic and have mild to severe postpartum depression. For women with nutritional abnormalities, psychosis, suicidality, and severe withdrawal symptoms, the use of electroconvulsive therapy can be entertained (89).

If medications are recommended for breast-feeding mothers, there is often the concern about the ability of these medications to show up in breast milk. Unfortunately, there are no research studies looking into the long-term effects on the brain and nervous system of infants exposed to antidepressants. Breast-fed infants exposed to antidepressants need extra monitoring for things like feeding difficulties, poor weight gain, sleep deficits, and developmental function.

The lowest effective dose should initially be prescribed with observation of the effects on both the mother and the infant. It is recommended to give the antidepressant immediately after nursing the infant and before the infant goes to sleep in order to lessen the infant's exposure to peak drug concentrations (90).

Women who are extra-sensitive to antidepressant medication side effects should be started on half of the recommended starting dose for four days, increasing the dose by small amounts until the women's symptoms are resolved. An acute response to the medication is considered successful when the mother's symptoms are reduced by half.

After there has been a response for about six to eight weeks, the dose should be maintained for at least six months in order to prevent relapse. The pediatrician should be involved when the mother takes an antidepressant and nurses her infant just as in cases of any medication given to a nursing mother. The pediatrician can monitor the baby for adverse side effects including changes in eating patterns, changes in sleep patterns, irritability, and sedation.

Hormone therapy has also been tried in the treatment of postpartum depression. Women given estradiol, for example, show a reduction in symptoms of depression in the first month after the baby's birth. This carries with it an increased risk of endometrial hyperplasia, deep vein thrombosis, and lowering of the amount of milk she produces. On the other hand, giving progesterone instead has been found to increase the rate of postpartum depression.

Alternative therapies have been tried, including acupuncture, the use of St. John's Wort, light therapy, massage therapy, and exercise. The results have been mixed but at least help promote awareness of postpartum depression and decrease the rate of underdiagnosing the disorder. Women who were identified and educated about postpartum depression sought treatment at a rate of 93.4 percent (91). This strongly supports the need for regular screening and education regarding postpartum depression.

Medications Available for Postpartum Depression

There are several classifications of medications used in the management of postpartum depression. The primary classification used includes the following SSRI medications:

- Sertraline (Zoloft)
- Citalopram (Celexa)
- Fluoxetine (Prozac)
- Escitalopram (Lexapro)

- Paroxetine (Paxil)
- Trazodone (Oleptro)
- Fluvoxamine (Luvox)

SSRIs are found to be extremely helpful in treating women with postpartum depression, and they cause few side effects, with sexual side effects being the most prevalent.

SNRI medications (serotonin and norepinephrine reuptake inhibitors) work by increasing the levels of both norepinephrine and serotonin in the brain. These include the following:

- Desvenlafaxine (Pristiq)
- Venlafaxine (Effexor XR)
- Duloxetine (Cymbalta)

Cymbalta not only treats postpartum depression but also is useful in the management of pain disorders.

Tricyclic antidepressants are older than the SSRI agents but can be prescribed if the SSRI medications don't seem to be effective. They carry more side effects, including dry mouth, constipation, and tiredness. Other side effects include seizures, abnormal heartbeat, and low blood pressure.

Tricyclic antidepressants include the following:

- Amoxipine (Asendin)
- Amitriptyline (Elavil)
- Clomipramine (Anafranil)
- Maprotiline (Ludiomil)
- Norpramin (Desipramine)
- Imipramine (Tofranil)
- Nortriptyline (Pamelor)
- Doxepin (Sinequan)
- Protriptyline (Vivactil)
- Trimipramine (Surmontil)

There is one tetracyclic antidepressant called maprotiline (Ludiomil) that is Category B and can be used for the management of postpartum depression associated with anxiety.

Bupropion (Wellbutrin) is a norepinephrine and dopamine blocker that can be used for postpartum depression and seasonal affective disorder. It is also used by individuals trying to quit smoking.

Monoamine oxidase inhibitors or MAOIs are older antidepressant medications that work by preventing the breakdown of serotonin, dopamine, and norepinephrine. They are harder for women to take because they have strong interactions with other prescription drugs, foods, and some nonprescription drugs. They also cannot be combined with other antidepressants and are therefore rarely a first-line treatment.

MAOIs include the following:

- Isocaboxazid (Marplan)
- Phenelzine (Nardil)
- Selegiline (Esam)
- Tranylcypromine (Parnate)

Whatever antidepressant is chosen, it should be assumed that it shows up in breast milk and that the infant may have adverse effects because of exposure to the medications. The risks versus the benefits of taking these types of medications in nursing mothers need to be discussed before she takes the drug.

If you go write a prescription for an antidepressant, think: bipolar/mood swings.

Someone with an underlying bipolar disorder can be flipped into mania when prescribed an antidepressant.

If the patient has gotten worse on antidepressants in the past, think bipolar.

Ask if they have ever attempted suicide in the past.

(See assessment of mood disorders)

I didn't want to leave my house for weeks... I didn't want my husband to leave for work each morning... I would beg him to stay home with me... I would call him every hour of the day... I had to have someone with me all of the time.

Chapter 18

TREATMENT OF POSTPARTUM ANXIETY

While becoming a mother is generally considered a meaningful and joyous experience, there are a number of sudden changes occurring during this time that giving birth is considered a stressful life event. About 10–20 percent of women of childbearing age will suffer from postpartum depression, and an unknown number of these women tend to suffer from anxiety along with depression or just anxiety symptoms without depression. The ramifications of not treating these psychiatric disorders after the birth of the child can have far-reaching implications for the mom, the infant, and the relationship the mother has with her partner (167).

Postpartum depression has received a great deal of clinical and research attention. However, anxiety and stress-related diseases has been largely ignored. Many doctors are using the Edinburgh Postnatal Depression Scale (EPDS) in order to detect the presence of postpartum depression in new mothers. Anxiety is often minimized or overlooked, especially when it occurs in the absence of underlying depression. For anxiety, the test that is often used is the Depression Anxiety Stress Scales or DASS-21.

Postpartum depression occurs at a higher rate than postpartum anxiety and other mood disorders, and for this reason, it has taken the lion's share of the research attention. Several researchers, however, have looked into the importance of identifying both postpartum depression and postpartum anxiety and recognizing the differences between the two (168). It is widely known that postpartum anxiety and postpartum depression exist together. It has more recently been found that anxiety alone in the postpartum state can cause problems with the mother-infant bond and therefore needs to be treated even if depression in the postpartum state does not exist.

One study (169) looked into the importance of telling the difference between depression and anxiety in the postpartum state in order to provide the appropriate treatment modalities for women with anxiety. According to the research, not all anxious mothers are also depressed. In addition, research with non-postpartum populations have reported that anxious depression (a comorbidity of anxiety and depression) has more severe symptoms and is harder to treat than each psychiatric disorder by itself (170). Having both disorders increases the chance for suicide and results in a worsened short- and long-term outcome.

The treatment of both disorders in most cases requires that the depression be treated first even when the anxiety symptoms are more prominent than the depressed features (167). The increased focus on depression can result in nondetection of the anxiety symptoms. This results in the anxiety not being treated.

> *My husband tells me it's my fault, if I would just relax*
> *and not be so anxious, this baby wouldn't be so irritable,*
> *and cry all the time. I don't know how to relax.*

> —*Anxious postpartum mom*

In the same way, when there are situations of anxiety and depression coexisting (also referred to as anxious depression), there is always a risk that the treatment focuses on the depression to the exclusion of the anxiety symptoms. In such cases, it is important to determine whether the anxiety is a part of the depressive disorder or is its own clinical diagnosis (171).

Anxiety in the postpartum state may, in fact, be a precursor to depression as a result of failing to manage the stress after delivery or from altered physiological pathways. Stress is a distinctive negative emotional condition that involves being chronically aroused and having impaired psychological function. In one sample of new moms, it was found that the levels of stress and poor coping responses led to depressive symptoms (172).

Measuring Postpartum Depression

There are several rating scales for depression that have been used on non-postpartum individuals. These rating scales have questionable validity when it comes to being used in the postpartum state. Some items in these scales, such as lack of sleep, weight loss, listlessness, and poor concentration, are felt to be normal findings among nursing mothers rather than being related to depression (172). Scales that use these types of symptoms may artificially increase the woman's depression scores, increasing the chance of having false positive test results.

Because of these possible confounding factors, the Edinburgh Postnatal Depression Scale (EPSD) was developed in 1987 by Cox, Holden, and Sagovsky (173). The EPSD questions are as follows:

In the past seven days,

1. I have been able to laugh and see the funny side of things.
2. I have looked forward with enjoyment to things.
3. I have blamed myself unnecessarily when things went wrong.
4. I have been anxious or worried for no good reason.
5. I have felt scared or panicky for no very good reason.
6. Things have been getting on top of me.
7. I have been so unhappy I have difficulty sleeping.
8. I have felt sad or miserable.
9. I have been so unhappy that I have been crying.
10. The thought of harming myself has occurred to me.

Women answer if they have had the symptoms most of the time, some of the time, not very often, or never. This test has proved to be very simple to administer, reliable, and user-friendly for the screening of women with postpartum depression in research studies and in clinical practice (175). While the test was originally designed to measure depression in postpartum women, it has been suggested that the EPDS is also a good test for anxiety.

Most studies on the Edinburgh Postpartum Depression Score use a score of over 12 to indicate the possible presence of depression. However, some scientists believe that a score of 9 or more is more sensitive when it comes to identifying depressive symptoms (176). Regardless of the cutoff scored used, a positive finding on the EPSD indicates that there is a need for further evaluation. The EPDS doesn't tell the difference between the different levels of depression, so more information is needed in order to identify the presence of depression in this population. Many studies have taken to using the Beck Depression Inventory along with the EPDS to identify exactly how severe the depression is in postpartum women.

The Depression Anxiety and Stress Scales

The core symptoms of depression, such as changes in appetite, weight changes, loss of libido, and sleep disturbances tend to be weak markers for depression. Using the Depression, Anxiety and Stress Scales (DASS), researchers have rejected items that have been identified as confounding variables in the Beck Depression Inventory in the postpartum state (177).

The DASS-21 Scale is as follows:

Over the past week,

1. I found it hard to wind down.
2. I was aware of dryness in my mouth.
3. I couldn't seem to experience any positive feelings at all.
4. I experienced breathing difficulty.
5. I found it difficult to work up the initiative to do things.
6. I tended to overreact to situations.
7. I experienced trembling.
8. I felt that I was using a lot of nervous energy.
9. I was worried about situations in which I might panic or make a fool of myself.
10. I felt that I had nothing to look forward to.
11. I found myself getting agitated.
12. I found it difficult to relax.
13. I felt downhearted and blue.
14. I was intolerant of anything that kept me from getting on with what I was doing.
15. I was close to panic.
16. I was unable to be enthusiastic about doing anything.
17. I felt I wasn't worth much as a person.
18. I felt that I was rather touchy.
19. I was aware of the action of my heart in the absence of physical exertion.
20. I felt scared without any good reason.
21. I felt that life was meaningless.

Women answered whether they felt these things not at all, some of the time, a good part of the time, or most of the time. There are items on the DASS-21 that are directly related to increased stress.

The DASS-21 has been found to distinguish reliably between the symptoms of depression, anxiety, and stress in nonclinical and clinical samples (178). The researchers recommend that the DASS-21 be used along with clinical interviews in order to identify anxiety and depression in the postpartum state.

My mother-in-law is driving me crazy, she wants to hold the baby all the time. What I really need is for her to do something. It's my baby. I dread seeing her car pull in the driveway. My husband says I'm making this all up. He tells me just get over it.

Looking at the Criteria for Postpartum Distress

The postpartum state represents one of the most important life stages in a woman's life for which the accurate detection and management of psychological distress is necessary. The transition from pregnancy to motherhood has been associated with an increase in emotional distress in as many as 30 percent of women (179).

Given the high potential for untreated postpartum anxiety and distress to adversely affect the well-being of the mother and her infant, it seems to make sense to distinguish the mother's negative emotions in order to treat her anxiety symptoms. The term "postnatal distress" can be used to identify stress, anxiety, and depression in the postpartum state. The DASS-21 is helpful because it can identify the three negative emotions as separate entities, it can identify the comorbidity of these negative emotions, and it does not include the confounding factors found in typical depression scales. It can identify the mild symptoms of each negative emotion in order to identify those women who might just be anxious.

Stressful life events such as childbirth and the introduction of a new family member have the potential to cause episodes of depression and anxiety and lead to a stress response that involves the mother being chronically aroused and suffering from impaired function. Given that being a new mother is a stressful life event, it is reasonable to assume that the DASS-21 can be used to detect the various emotional states a woman might be in, including anxiety, depression, and stress.

In one study (180), researchers looked into the prevalence of postpartum distress among a group of postpartum women and looked at the use of the EPDS along with the DASS-21 to identify anxiety states. They also looked into the extent to which mothers who were stressed and anxious might have been missed when the researchers used the criteria for depression alone. They also looked at the comorbidity of anxiety and depression, with particular interest in those women who had a combination of anxiety and depression (anxious depression) as well as the extent to which the EPDS alone detected this type of situation.

The study invited first-time moms to participate in the study. In order to eliminate factors related to having more than one child, only women who were first-time moms were included. The women were between six weeks postpartum and six months postpartum when invited to the study.

A total of three hundred twenty five women participated in the study, ranging from eighteen to forty-four years of age. The babies ranged in age from six weeks to six months. Ninety-four percent of participants were married or in a relationship, while 2.8 percent were in a noncohabitating relationship. A total of 1.5 percent were single at the time of the study.

The DASS-21 consists of three self-report scales that have been designed to measure depression, stress, and anxiety. The depression scale measures things like hopelessness, dysphoria, devaluation of life, lack of interest/involvement, inertia, self-deprecation, and inertia. The anxiety scale measures skeletal muscle effects, autonomic arousal, situational anxiety, and the subjective experience of anxiety. The stress part of the scale measures nervous arousal, being easily upset or agitated, irritability, impatience, and difficulty relaxing. The original DASS test had twenty-one items, but it has since been shortened to a briefer DASS-21 test. In the DASS-21 test, there are seven questions each regarding depression, anxiety, and stress.

The EPDS was designed to screen postpartum women for an increased likelihood of having postnatal depression. It addresses things like anhedonia, reactivity, self-blame, panic, anxiety, coping, insomnia related to unhappiness, tearfulness, sadness, and harm to the self. It excluded the somatic symptoms because they can normally be found in the postpartum state in women who are not depressed.

The postpartum women had a mean EPDS score of 6.94 and identified thirty-six women who had a score greater than the usually recommended cutoff of 12. Using the more sensitive value of 9, however, 25 percent of women were identified as probably depressed. Those with a score of 9 or less were identified as not likely to be depressed. The DASS-21 depression scale was used to identify the severity of the depression noted.

The average DASS-21 depression score was 5.21. The average DASS-21 anxiety score was 3.33, and the average DASS-21 stress score was 10. This resulted in five severity categories, being "normal, mild, moderate, severe, and extremely severe." Those who scored normal were considered not to be depressed, and those who scored in the other categories were considered to be depressed to some degree. The number of women identified as depressed was 19 percent.

The DASS-21 scale looked at anxiety and stress as well as depression. Women were ranked in the above severity categories with respect to anxiety and stress as well. For example, those who scored normal in the anxiety scale were identified as being not anxious, and those who scored normal in the stress scale were found to be not stressed.

According to the DASS-21, forty-six women were found to be depressed, while thirty-four women were found not to be depressed. Of the thirty-four women identified by the EPDS as likely depressed but who didn't show depression on the DASS-21 scale, ten were found to be anxious, and five were found to be stressed. Women who scored in the mild moderate, severe, or extremely severe categories on at least one DASS-21 subscale were considered to be suffering from postpartum distress.

Of the total number of women (325 total), 28 percent were distressed. Of these, 64 percent were depressed, 19 percent were anxious, and 16 percent were stressed. Had depression been the only criterion assessed, a total of thirty-three distressed women (more than 10 percent of the total) would have been missed as having difficulties in the postpartum period.

The findings indicated that despite the sensitivity of the EPDS (using a cutoff of 9), fourteen depressed women were not identified by the test as likely to be depressed, and eighteen women who were distressed in the postpartum state would not have been further assessed if the EPDS were the only screening tool used. Thirteen percent of women had isolated anxiety or anxiety in combination with either depression or stress.

Interestingly, the EPDS (a tool to identify depressed women) was able to identify ten out of eighteen women who were anxious but not depressed. It also detected five cases of stress in the absence of depression.

Overall, the study identified a broader classification for postnatal distress to include measures of anxiety, stress, and depression as separate but intermingling entities. It pointed out the need for a broader assessment of distress in the postpartum state in order to provide early intervention for those women who don't meet the criteria for depression but are instead anxious or stressed about their life circumstances after giving birth.

Another study (181) looked at a community-based group of 107 women who completed the Beck Anxiety Inventory, the State-Trait Anxiety Inventory, the Beck Depression Inventory, and the EODS at fourteen weeks after their delivery and at thirty weeks after their delivery. The prevalence of anxiety was about 9 percent at fourteen weeks and about 17 percent at thirty weeks postpartum. The prevalence of depression was 23 percent at fourteen weeks and 19 percent at thirty weeks postpartum. The study suggested that the Edinburgh Postnatal Depression Scale might be a good screening tool for both anxiety and depression in the postpartum state.

I get so anxious, heart beats so fast, I think I'm dying, I'm afraid I will drop her, so I change her on the floor because I can't go upstairs with her.

—*Anxious postpartum mother*

Medications for Anxiety in the Postpartum State

Bearing in mind that almost all medications for anxiety are secreted in breast milk, the following medications can be used for postpartum anxiety in nonbreast-feeding mothers or in those who have anxiety that is so severe as to require treatment despite the breast-feeding status. Some good medications for anxiety include the following:

Benzodiazepines

- alprazolam (Xanax) (this the most addictive benzodiazepine, with the shortest half-life)
- clonazepam (Klonopin)
- diazepam (Valium)
- lorazepam (Ativan)
- oxazepam (Serax)
- chlordiazepoxide (Librium)

Beta Blockers

- propranolol (Inderal)
- atenolol (Tenormin)

Tricyclic Antidepressants

- imipramine (Tofranil)
- desipramine (Norpramin)
- nortriptyline (Pamelor)
- amitriptyline (Elavil)
- doxepin (Sinequan)
- clomipramine (Anafranil)

Other Antidepressants

- trazodone (Desyrel)

Monoamine Oxidase Inhibitors

- phenelzine (Nardil)
- tranylcypromine (Parnate)

Selective Serotonin Reuptake Inhibitors (SSRIs)

- fluoxetine (Prozac)
- fluvoxamine (Luvox)
- sertraline (Zoloft)
- paroxetine (Paxil)
- escitalopram (Lexapro)
- citalopram (Celexa)

Serotonin Norepinephrine Reuptake Inhibitors (SNRIs)

- venlafaxine (Effexor)
- duloxetine (Cymbalta)
- desvenlafaxine (Prisitq)

Mild Tranquilizer

- busipirone (BuSpar)

Anticonvulsants

- valproate (Depakote)
- pregabalin (Lyrica)
- gabapentin (Neurontin)

The medications should be given in the lowest effective dose and should be given with the idea that the woman might be breast-feeding while suffering from anxiety.

If you go to write a prescription for an antidepressant,
think: bipolar/mood swings.
Someone with an underlying bipolar disorder can be flipped into mania when prescribed antidepressant.

If the patient has gotten worse on antidepressants in the past, think bipolar. Ask if they have ever attempted suicide in the past.
(See assessment of mood disorders)

Psychotherapy

In women who are breast-feeding or who refuse to take medications for anxiety, psychotherapy may be recommended. In such cases, the woman can undergo cognitive behavioral therapy or another type of therapy that addresses the issues a woman might face in the immediate postpartum state as she tries to juggle parenthood and the necessary life changes that go with it.

Chapter 19

TREATMENT OF POST
PARTUM PSYCHOSIS

Postpartum psychosis occurs in approximately one to two out of every one thousand women of childbearing age. It generally begins within the first two to four weeks after delivery and has a rapid onset (182). The affected woman suffers from the following symptoms:

- Mood swings
- Confused thoughts
- Paranoid, grandiose, or bizarre delusions
- Hallucinations
- Disorganized behavior

Fortunately, postpartum psychosis is much less common compared with the incidence of postpartum depression (at 10–25 percent) and baby blues, which affects 50–75 percent of women who have recently given birth. On the other hand, the lapse in judgment and psychotic behavior in women can lead to devastating outcomes in which both the well-being and safety of the mother and baby are compromised (183). This means that it is vital to quickly recognize and treat these symptomatic and sometimes dangerous patients.

While the DSM-V classifies postpartum psychosis as nothing more than a serious form of major depression or the onset of a primary psychotic disorder (such as schizophrenia), there are data to suggest that postpartum depression is actually a severe form of bipolar disorder after giving birth (184). Of patients who developed postpartum psychosis following the birth, about 72–88 percent have bipolar disorder, while only about 12 percent had a prior history of schizophrenia.

Factors that may contribute to the onset of postpartum psychosis include the following:

- Hormone shifts after delivery
- Complications of the birth
- Increased environmental stress
- Sleep deprivation.

In this chapter, we will talk about postpartum psychosis so that you can recognize the symptoms of the disease, evaluate the condition and quickly refer the patient for psychiatric care. The patient and her family will need to learn as much as possible about this condition.

In one study (185), the classical findings in a postpartum mother with postpartum depression were found to be the following:

- Withdrawn state
- Auditory hallucinations
- Unusual affect
- Incompetency in child-rearing
- Confusion
- Catatonia
- Moods that alternate between elation and depression
- Rambling speech
- Agitation
- Excessive activity

The unusual beliefs might focus on themes related to childbirth or concern that the baby has a changed identity. The woman may feel persecuted by her infant, often described as a "changeling." Many women suffer from delusions of reference, jealousy, grandiosity, and persecution that are unrelated to their mood. The woman may have tactile, olfactory, and visual hallucinations, which suggest that the condition is organic in nature (186). The average age at onset is about twenty-six years, which is the time when most women are delivering their first or second child. When compared with women suffering from a chronic mental illness, patients with postpartum psychosis have usually attained higher functional abilities prior to the onset of their psychosis.

The average risk rate for postpartum psychosis is about one in five hundred births. This risk increases to about one out of seven women who have had a past episode of postpartum depression (182). Women suffering from postpartum psychosis or who had a first degree relative with the disease have a chance of getting the disease by a factor of more than 74 percent. Women with bipolar disorder or schizoaffective disorder have a better than half chance of getting postpartum psychosis. Women with bipolar disorder who have no family history of postpartum psychosis have only about a 30 percent chance of getting the disease.

Patients who discontinue their mood stabilizer (especially lithium) are more likely to have a recurrence of bipolar disorder or postpartum psychosis (70 percent) when compared to women who remain on medications to control mania (24 percent). Those mothers who stop their mood stabilizers are at a greater risk of a bipolar relapse (187).

Things like marital discord, environmental stressors, sleep deprivation, and a significant loss of hormone levels after giving birth are typical factors related to getting postpartum depression. Things like being a first-time mother, ethnicity, and socioeconomic status play a lesser role (188). This means that healthcare providers must play a role in identifying the emergency of symptoms related to postpartum psychosis, especially when it comes to postpartum psychosis in mothers who have a preexisting case of bipolar disorder and in those who have a personal or family history of the disease.

In the first year following childbirth, the rate of suicide increases by seventyfold. In fact, suicide is the leading cause of death in women within a year of delivery (189). Fortunately, of one thousand women with postpartum psychosis, only about two complete their suicide. The women who were successful in committing suicide were more likely to have irreversible means of committing suicide, such as jumping from a great height or self-incineration, compared with mothers who just took an overdose.

It is therefore crucial that health care providers and health professionals get a handle on the safety of their patient by asking about suicidal ideation, including feelings that life is not worth living, thoughts of dying, plans to commit suicide, past suicide attempts, and access to weapons. In such cases, suicidal ideation must be taken seriously. Patients with an active suicidal plan should be referred to psychiatry in an emergency setting.

Fortunately, homicidal behavior rarely occurs in postpartum psychosis. Among women hospitalized for postpartum depression, only about 28–35 percent of these women had delusions surrounding their babies, but only 9 percent had actual thoughts of doing harm to the infant (190). Women with postpartum psychosis are, however, more likely to have homicidal thinking compared with women who have nonpsychotic disorders after delivery.

The cognitive distortions that occur in postpartum depression can result in a mother being neglectful of her infant's needs and may practice unsafe techniques when caring for their infant (191). This makes it vital to ask a mother with postpartum psychosis about any type of homicidal thoughts she may have and to get the aid of social services and psychiatric care in order to prevent harm to the mother or other members of her family.

The terms "infanticide" and "neonaticide" are different in nature. Women with neonaticide often suffer from dissociative states. They often denied their pregnancy and felt no pain during the birth of their child. They often experienced symptoms of depersonalization, brief amnesia, and dissociative hallucinations. These mothers may refuse to attend prenatal visits and may deliver at home without the benefit of medical attention. They often abandon their infants shortly after giving birth. Neonaticide is more difficult to prevent because it involves the woman denying her pregnancy in the first place (192).

Prognosis of Postpartum Psychosis

Many studies have indicated that there is a good prognosis for many women with postpartum psychosis coming out of a bipolar disorder (193). About 75–86 percent were free of symptoms after an episode of postpartum depression. For women with schizophrenia, about half remained healthy after an episode of postpartum depression, while greater than a third will develop recurrent postpartum depression, and 5 percent have a difficult illness course, with many episodes of psychotic symptoms with and without being in the postpartum state.

Those women who sought psychiatric help within a month of the child's birth had a more favorable course and were less likely to suffer from long-term illness (13 percent) compared with women who sought help after a month following the birth (33 percent) (194). Compared with women who had a new diagnosis of non-postpartum psychosis, those women with a first episode of postpartum psychosis suffered from higher levels of disorientation and confusion but only needed half the time to achieve a response to treatment.

I went into the kitchen... I would see the knives... and picture them stabbing the baby... I would look at the microwave and see the baby in the oven... The sink and the baby drowning in the water... Then the pictures changed... And suddenly it was me doing the hurting...

—Postpartum mom

Screening for Postpartum Psychosis

Those women with a known case of bipolar disorder and a family or personal history of having postpartum depression are at greater risk of developing postpartum depression during the current postpartum state. The family and mother should be warned of the potential symptoms to recognize in the first two to four weeks after the delivery, in particular:

- Confusion
- Mood Swings
- Hallucinations
- Unusual beliefs

If any of these symptoms occur, psychiatric help should be looked for. The woman at risk for postpartum psychosis may need a consultation with a psychiatrist prior to her delivery in order to consider the various treatment options or the starting of treatment at the time of delivery in order to avoid symptoms (184). If this isn't done, obstetricians and others who deliver babies should ask about the symptoms of postpartum psychosis in those patients who are at high risk for the disease during the six-week postdelivery follow-up visit.

Screening tools that are especially helpful include the Edinburgh Postnatal Depression Scale and the Mood Disorder Questionnaire (195). The Mood Disorder Questionnaire is a "yes-no" questionnaire that includes the following:

1. Has there ever been a period of time when you were not your usual self and

- you felt so good or hyper that other people thought you were not your normal self, or you were so hyper that you got into trouble?
- you were so irritable that you shouted at people or started fights or arguments?
- you felt more self-confident than usual?
- you got much less sleep than usual and found you didn't really miss it?
- you were much more talkative or spoke much faster than usual?
- you had thoughts racing through your mind or couldn't slow your mind down?
- you were so easily distracted by things around you that you had trouble concentrating or staying on track?
- you had much more energy than usual.
- you were much more active or did many more things than usual?
- you were much more social or outgoing than usual, such as telephoning your friends in the middle of the night?
- you were much more interested in sex than usual?
- you did things that were unusual for you or that other people might have thought were excessive, foolish, or risky?

- you spent money that got you or a family into trouble?

2. If you answered *yes* to more than one of the above, have several of these ever happened during the same period of time?
3. How much of a problem did any of these cause you, such as being unable to work; having family, money, or legal troubles; getting into arguments or fights?
4. Have any of your blood relatives had manic depressive illness or bipolar disorder?
5. Has a health professional ever told you that you have manic depressive illness or bipolar disorder?

If the patient answered *yes* to seven or more of the items under question 1 and *yes* to question 2 and answered "moderate" or "serious" to question 3, this represents a positive screen for a bipolar mood disorder. All three of the above criteria should be positive for the disorder.

The Mood Disorder Questionnaire looks for past and current symptoms of elevated, irritable, or hyper mood, racing thoughts, excessive energy, pressured speech, and symptoms related to having hypomania or mania. Whenever the patient reports being confused, expresses difficulty caring for her children, threatens to harm herself or others, or exhibits poor self-care, the health care provider must consider these suspicious for postpartum depression and should quickly arrange for a referral to psychiatry.

Differential Diagnosis

Postpartum depression is to be considered a psychiatric emergency that requires urgent medical evaluation, psychiatric referral, and possibly an admission to the hospital (196). There needs to be a thorough psychiatric history, laboratory evaluations, and physical examination that excludes an organic cause for the psychosis. Some tests to run include the following:

- CBC
- Electrolytes
- BUN
- Creatinine
- Glucose
- Vitamin B12
- Folate
- Thyroid function studies
- Calcium
- Urinalysis

- Urine culture if symptomatic
- Urine drug screen

Sometimes, a head CT or MRI can be ordered in order to rule out an ischemic stroke from occlusion or hemorrhage (197). The stroke patient often has different symptoms than the patient with simple postpartum depression, including severe headache, preeclampsia, hypertension, unilateral weakness, fluid and electrolyte imbalance, sensory deficits, or seizures.

The main differential diagnosis to be made in early onset postpartum psychosis is bipolar disorder. About 95 percent of postpartum cases also fulfilled the diagnostic criteria for a cyclic mood disorder at a five-year follow-up test (198). Of these cases, half were misdiagnosed when they first presented with symptoms.

Postpartum psychosis and bipolar psychosis share the same symptoms, so it is natural to expect a misdiagnosis. These symptoms include the following:

- Dysphoria
- Elation
- Mood lability
- Confusion
- Heightened sensitivity
- Sleep deprivation

Women with a past history or family history of bipolar disorder precipitates an attack of postpartum psychosis. These patients usually require medication against mania. Assuming they are not breast-feeding, take into consideration sedation so the mom can hear the baby and respond. Some of the choices of mania management include the following:

- Lithium carbonate (weight gain)
- Valproate (Depakote) (weight gain and dysthymic depression)
- Carbamazepine (Tegretol) (potential drop in white cell count)
- Olanzapine (Zyprexia) (sedating and can cause weight gain)
- Quetiapine (Seroquel) (sedating and can cause weight gain)
- Ziprasidone (Geodon)
- Aripiprazole (Abilify)
- Palperidone (Invega) (sedating and can cause weight gain and increased prolactin level)
- Risperidone (Risperdal) (sedating and can cause weight gain and increased prolactin level)
- Lurasidone (Latuda) (can cause sedation at higher doses)
- Iloperidone (Fanapt) (not a first-line medication because of QTC prolongation)
- Asenapine (Saphris)

Patients with postpartum psychosis can be differentiated from those with postpartum depression by the presence of cognitive disturbance, delusional beliefs, and disorganized behavior. On the other hand, women who have had a history of unipolar psychotic depression can relapse shortly after delivery and can develop postpartum depression (199). These patients often report the following symptoms:

- Distraught feelings about an inability to enjoy their infant
- Low mood
- Pacing behaviors
- Psychomotor slowing
- Anxiety
- Fatigue
- Poor concentration
- Preoccupation with unusual ideas
- Unusual suspicions

Can you tell my other kid over there in the corner to be quiet she's gonna wake up the baby. It's weird I know my daughters at home but I can see her over there in the corner and she's making noise. I want to tell anybody can think I'm nuts. Am I crazy? Maybe if I just ignore shall go away. Tell her to just be quiet.

Psychotic postpartum mom

Without some type of intervention, these patients are at risk for death, treatment resistance, and worsening of their symptoms (200). They respond best to antidepressant medications as well as antipsychotic drug treatment or ECT.

Postpartum psychosis must also be distinguished from obsessive-compulsive disorder (OCD). When a woman has obsessive-compulsive symptoms, she usually has the following symptoms:

- Feelings about contamination
- Fear over causing harm to their baby
- Offensive or violent images
- Sexual images
- Urges for symmetry
- Religious preoccupation

They also develop certain compulsions, such as urges to check things, urges to clean, need for order, need to repeat things, hoarding rituals, and other mental rituals (like counting). Women who have postpartum depression often have obsessive compulsive symptoms at a rate of about 41–57 percent (201). These are often the most distressing to the mother.

The difference between obsessive compulsive disorder and postpartum depression is that those with OCD usually preserve reality testing and rational judgment. They may have aggressive thoughts, but they don't act on them. They avoid those objects or places that provoke a sense of anxiety and are uncomfortable about their unwanted thoughts. On the other hand, patients with postpartum psychosis are unable to identify reality, can't assess the consequences of what they do, and feel compelled to act on their delusions (202).

The main treatments for obsessive compulsive disorder in the postpartum state includes SSRI therapy, such as fluoxetine, sertraline, and fluvoxamine. The gold standard treatment is clomipramine, which is both a serotonin reuptake inhibitor and a norepinephrine inhibitor. Most patients require cognitive behavioral therapy along with medications. If the patient has refractory OCD, they may need to be treated with an atypical antipsychotic drug.

Postpartum psychosis can also be representative of a preexisting or new onset psychotic disorder, such as schizophrenia. Women with a past history of schizophrenia are at risk of postpartum exacerbations by a factor of 25 percent increase (203). Other studies have shown a low prevalence of schizophrenia in women with early onset postpartum psychosis (about 3.4–4.5 percent). These patients tend to be good responders to medications like atypical antipsychotic drugs. If depression is suspected, an antidepressant is added. Mothers who have a history of schizophrenia may also benefit from referral to home care for added support and for the enhancement of their skills in parenting.

I kept hearing voices to kill the children so that they could be in a safer, better place... with God.

—*Andrea Yates*

When the diagnosis of postpartum psychosis is made, the health care provider should do the following:

- Rule out organic causes of the symptoms
- Educate the patient and her family about the illness
- Start giving the woman medications
- Continue to assess the patient's functionality and safety

Informing the patient and family about the symptoms, therapy, and prognosis of postpartum psychosis can greatly enhance the therapeutic alliance with the family and will strengthen the mother's decision-making about the possibilities for treatment as well as her feelings of mastery and self-efficacy (204).

After the patient has been stabilized and has begun taking medications for postpartum psychosis, there should be a carefully designed discharge plan before the patient can leave the hospital. Intensive outpatient therapy can be started, or a referral to a day program can be initiated. There should be follow-up visits, especially in the first several weeks after the patient leaves the hospital. This can facilitate the ne mother's return to her home and will allow for close monitoring of the treatment plan and outcome of therapy.

For example, sleep deprivation is a major precipitator of postpartum psychosis and mania in the postpartum state. Health care providers can help by encouraging the family to gain the help of others, including family, friends, or a doula so the mother can have a better chance to sleep. Patients and their families should be advised to speak to the doctor as soon as symptoms reoccur (205). Doctors or other health care providers should look at the patient's adherence to therapy and look for evidence of side effects to the medications, adjusting the dose or switching the medications if necessary.

Some kind of supportive psychotherapy just before hospital discharge can include teaching the mother parenting skills and can address early infant interventions that attack the maternal-infant bond. In-home services can be invaluable and can affect outcomes. Other psychotherapy options besides cognitive behavioral therapy include the following:

- Family-focused therapy
- Interpersonal therapy (IPT)

Both of these can be effective therapies for postpartum mood disorders. IPT has been adapted for the postpartum state and is structured to help those women who are undergoing role changes, relationship issues, and perceived losses. These types of psychotherapy are relatively advanced and are recommended once the patient as regained more organized thinking.

Drug Therapy for Postpartum Psychosis

Pharmacotherapy with drugs designed to manage postpartum psychosis is important in the management of both the psychotic symptoms and mood-related symptoms seen in the disorder. Medication choices include mood stabilizers, atypical antipsychotic agents, and antiepileptic drugs (206). Some women can be satisfactorily managed on just one medication, while others require several different medications in order to control their symptoms and cause remission. Side effects can be minimized by starting at low doses and titrating upward in order to get the desired response. Using genetic testing can make this process significantly easier (see the chapter on psychiatric pharmacogenomics).

Breast-feeding Issues

The mother may wish to breast-feed. In such cases, the benefits and risks need to be considered by the doctor and the breast-feeding mother (207). Fortunately, the American Academy of Pediatrics has several helpful recommendations regarding breast-feeding and the use of lithium or antiepileptic medications. The pediatrician must be informed if the mother wishes to breast-feed so that he or she can monitor the breastfed infant. Mothers also need to look out for behavioral changes suggestive of toxicity to the infant, including the following:

- Sedation
- Poor hydration
- Poor feeding
- Poor weight gain
- Blood disorders
- Hepatic dysfunction

Breast-feeding mothers should be instructed to contact their children's doctor immediately when these symptoms are noted (207). Breast milk exposure can remain small if the prescribing doctor follows these recommendations:

1. Using the lowest-effective dose of the medication or medications
2. Using fewer drugs in order to achieve the best response
3. Dividing the doses during the day in order to avoid high serum concentrations when the mother takes the drug at one time during the day

Lithium for Postpartum Psychosis

Lithium can be a good treatment option when it comes to preventing and treating postpartum psychosis and preventing bipolar disorder symptoms. Women who have had postpartum psychosis in the past have better outcomes when the lithium treatment begins right after the delivery of the infant (208). Starting lithium in the third trimester is a bit more controversial. Among women who stop lithium have a greater risk of relapse (52 percent) when compared with women who continue their prophylactic treatment (21 percent). If the patient is already taking lithium, she should be discouraged from stopping the drug abruptly. Treatment should be resumed as soon as she delivers.

When the woman is taking lithium for the treatment of postpartum psychosis, their kidney and thyroid function should be checked after the first five days of treatment. The target level of lithium is between 0.4 and 1.0 mEq/l at twelve hours after the last dose. Drug levels should be assessed every six to twelve months, even when the patient has become stable. Side effects to look out for include the following:

- Tremor
- Sedation
- Kidney dysfunction
- Nausea
- Vomiting
- Weight gain

There is a very small window between therapeutic levels of lithium and toxic levels of the drug. Things like thiazide diuretics, nonsteroidal anti-inflammatory drugs, and ACE inhibitors can interfere with the taking of lithium (209). Women suffering from dehydration are at a particularly high risk of becoming toxic on lithium. Physicians must watch carefully for symptoms of toxicity when taking lithium. These include the following:

- Excessive sedation
- Severe tremors
- Intractable vomiting
- Acute renal failure

A medication level should confirm the presence of lithium toxicity, and toxicity should be treated immediately by discontinuing the medication, hydrating the patient, and monitoring both the electrolyte balance and kidney function.

Lithium is not usually prescribed for breast-feeding women; however, its avoidance has been based on minimal data from decades ago (210). The concentration of lithium in breast-fed infants whose mothers are taking lithium is quickly toxic in neonates and young infants, who often develop fever, feeding difficulties, or dehydration. Lithium levels are about half of the therapeutic blood concentration. For this reason, the American Academy of Pediatrics advises strict caution in breast-feeding mothers who take lithium. If the patient insists on taking lithium and breast-feeding, a psychiatrist should be consulted with who has managed postpartum psychiatric illnesses.

Antiepileptic Drugs

Valproate (Depakote) is one drug that is FDA approved for bipolar disorder. The initial dose is 500–750 mg/day. The dose is titrated according to symptom response and the levels of the drug in the serum. Levels should be checked within a week of starting valproate. There should be monitoring of the following things whenever the dose is adjusted or toxicity suspected:

- Serum concentration of valproate
- Liver function studies
- Platelet count
- Glucose level
- Lipid profile

Therapeutic levels of valproate range from 50–125 µg/ml. If the levels are higher than that, side effects are more prominent. Side effects from taking valproate include the following:

- Nausea
- Tremor
- Weight gain
- Ataxia
- Diarrhea
- Abdominal pain
- Hepatitis
- Alopecia
- Thrombocytopenia
- Pancreatitis

Some women will experience polycystic ovarian syndrome, anovulation, menstrual irregularity, and insulin resistance when taking valproate (211).

Carbamazepine (Tegretol) is also FDA approved for the management of mania. Therapeutic doses are between 400 and 1699 mg/day. After starting the drug, a blood test is needed to identify a therapeutic level (4–12 µg/mL). Serum levels of the drug, liver function studies, and a CBC are necessary to do about two to three times a year in patients who are symptomatic and at least one per year if patients are on maintenance doses without symptoms. Side effects of carbamazepine include the following:

- Hepatitis
- Thrombocytopenia

- Leukopenia
- Rash
- Ataxia
- Sedation

One should not take carbamazepine and clozapine together because of the risk of bone marrow suppression that has been reported when they are taken together.

The American Academy of Pediatrics Committee on Drugs considers both valproate and carbamazepine to be compatible with breast-feeding. There have been cases of hepatic toxicity and cholestatic hepatitis in newborns exposed to the drug in utero and while breast-feeding (212). In most cases, no adverse side effects are noted in the infant exposed to the drug. Signs of toxicity include increased sedation, hematological impairment, liver impairment, and poor feeding.

Other antiepileptic drugs that have been FDA approved for bipolar disorder include oxcarbazepine and lamotrigine. Lamotrigine (Lamictal) must be titrated upward slowly to avoid a toxic skin side effect.

Oxcarbazepine (Trileptal) is usually given in divided doses, with a dosage range between 600 and 1200 mg/day. Side effects include lowered birth control efficacy, hyponatremia, and hypersensitivity reactions. Other side effects include the following:

- Dizziness
- Headache
- Gait imbalance
- Poor concentration
- Fatigue
- Memory alterations

It also appears that oxcarbazepine is secreted in breast milk in small amounts (213).

Lamotrigine is usually indicated for treatment of bipolar depression. The importance of gradual titration of the drug means that it is not usually appropriate for the management of acute psychotic states. It causes a nonserious rash in about 7–10 percent of cases and sometimes induces Stevens-Johnson syndrome, which is potentially life-threatening (this occurs in three out of one thousand patients taking the drug). A more serious rash is much more likely when the dose is increased rapidly or when taken in combination with valproate. The patient who gets a rash must stop the medication immediately and seek the advice of their doctor or psychiatrist (214).

The medication readily transfers to breast milk, and the serum drug level decrease is noticeably slower in infants and newborns. This means that this medication is not advisable for breast-feeding mothers shortly following the birth of their infant.

Atypical Antipsychotic Medications

The usual medications described as being atypical antipsychotic medications include olanzapine, risperidone, quetiapine, ziprasidone, aripiprazole, asenapine, clozaril, ilopridone, and lurisidone. All are indicated for the management of schizophrenia, bipolar mania, and acute psychosis. The dosages are as follows:

- Olanzapine (Zyprexa) 2.5–10 mg per day
- Risperidone (Risperdal) 2–6 mg per day
- Quetiapine (Seroquel) 25–700 mg per day
- Ziprasidone (Geodon) 20–80 mg twice daily
- Aripiprazole (Abilify) 10–15 mg in the morning
- Lurasidone (Latuda) 40–160 mg per day with food (at least 350 calories increases absorption)
- Asenapine (Saphris) 10–20 mg sublingual twice a day
- Iloperidone (Fanapt) 12–24 mg divided dose, titrate slowly to reduce orthostatic hypotension)
- Clozapine (Clozaril) 25–900 mg per day with slow titration
- Brexpiprazole (Rexulti) 2–4 mg per day increased death with breast-feeding)
- Cariprazine (Vraylar)1.5–6 mg per day

Common side effects include dry mouth, sleepiness, akathisia, and increase liver enzymes. Risperidone has been associated with hyperprolactinemia in 88 percent of cases. This compares with only 48 percent when taking haloperidol and minimal amounts in olanzapine (215). Patients who take these drugs are at risk for new onset metabolic syndrome, weight gain, and elevated triglycerides.

There should be close monitoring of glucose levels and lipid profiles when a woman is taking the drug. The patient should be encouraged to eat healthy, modify their diet, get regular exercise, and receive dietary counseling to minimize the effects of the drug on their body. Although extrapyramidal side effects like rigidity, tremor, bradykinesia, akathisia, dystonia, and tardive dyskinesia are rarely reported, there is a risk of these symptoms in the elderly, among women, and in those with affective disorders.

There are few cases of atypical antipsychotic exposures in infants who are breast-feeding. One woman in a single study (216) took olanzapine at 10 mg/day in the second and third trimester of pregnancy and continued to take the treatment during breast-feeding. The infant levels were undetectable even though the maternal levels were therapeutic. The infant was followed up to eleven months and continued to have normal weight, height, and head circumference. Tracking infant drug levels may be a good way to estimate the extent of the drug exposure and disposition in the nursing infant.

Infants taking risperidone through breast milk also had little in the way of serum concentration of the drug. The same was true in infants taking in quetiapine. The data suggest that exposure to these medications in breast-feeding is markedly less than their exposure in utero. Infants who are exposed through breast milk should still be monitored for sedation, feeding difficulties, hydration, and failure to gain weight. These are all signs of possible toxicity in the infant. Those who prescribe these medications to nursing mothers can reduce drug exposure by the infant by selecting the lowest-effective dose, dividing daily doses, and avoiding taking more than one drug at a time.

I hear sounds or voices when no one is around...

—Postpartum woman

Electroconvulsive Therapy

Before ECT was used in the management of postpartum psychosis, there was significant mortality associated with the disease. In 1927–1941, for example, nine out of fourteen women admitted to the hospital for postpartum psychosis died (217). The mortality rate dropped dramatically when ECT became used as a mainstream treatment of postpartum psychosis.

Women with postpartum psychosis responded better and faster when using ETC to treat their mood and psychotic symptoms compared with women who did not have postpartum psychosis (218). In one study, women with postpartum psychosis and psychotic bipolar depression had a greater than 50 percent improvement in depression, psychosis, and mania when treated with bilateral ECT. ECT seems to work especially well on women who have been admitted to the hospital with acute psychosis. It also works in those who have failed on medication therapy or in situations where the patient cannot wait for the delayed effects of antipsychotic medication.

Other Options

Researchers have looked into the possibility of replacing estrogen as a treatment for mental illness in the postpartum state. Its use so far is strictly investigational. There have been studies that suggest estrogen can prevent and treat postpartum psychosis in selected women who were hospitalized during the experiment and who were provided with antithrombotic therapy (219). The levels of estrogen seen before treatment were similar to the levels seen in menopausal women. After estrogen treatment, the women had a rapid resolution of psychosis, mood, and cognitive symptoms. Their treatment response correlated with a restoration of normal estrogen levels more appropriate to premenopausal women. Other studies have failed to corroborate these findings.

There are no specific treatment guidelines for the treatment of postpartum psychosis. Once medical causes of acute psychosis have been eliminated, the first-line drug treatment should be based upon what the underlying diagnosis is. Those with postpartum psychosis and who have a known bipolar disorder or family members with the disease are likely having an episode of bipolar disorder and will benefit from taking lithium, an antiepileptic drug or an atypical antipsychotic medication.

Women who have had a diagnosis of schizophrenia that has relapsed in the postpartum state usually benefit from some type of atypical antipsychotic medication. The exact medication chosen should depend on their history of past treatments and their responsiveness to those treatments.

Conclusion

The main features of postpartum psychosis include an early and rapid onset of disease associated with delusional beliefs, extreme confusion, mood swings, and an inability to function compared with baseline levels. The period of psychosis is usually brief, and there is a lack of long-term effects when treated quickly. Many have an underlying affective disorder, such as bipolar disorder. The prognosis is good as long as there hasn't been a premorbid psychosis in the past. Postpartum psychosis and postpartum bipolar disorder are distinct from more serious forms of bipolar disorder, manifesting as having recurrent attacks of mixed mania, bipolar psychosis, and refractory bipolar depression. These are associated with less-promising outcomes.

Clearly, more data need to be gathered from studies on the treatment and outcomes of women with postpartum psychosis compared with healthy women. There needs to be studies on the physical and neurodevelopmental outcomes of drug exposures in breast-fed infants. Persistent mental disorders have been linked with problems in infant-mother bonding. There needs to be a comparison between treating the disease and the outcomes that come out of not treating the disease.

I have spent the last 10 years of my career worrying about the impact of medications. I've been wrong. I should have been worrying more about the impact of the illness.

—*Dr. Zachary Stowe, Emory University-Atlanta,*
Neuropsychiatry Reviews, *June 2001*

Chapter 20

POST PARTUM DEPRESSION

AND LACTATION

For many decades, researchers on depression and breast-feeding have believed there is a connection between postpartum depression and breast-feeding. It has been felt that there was some protection against postpartum depression among women who breast-feed as well as an indication that stopping breast-feeding might trigger postpartum anxiety or postpartum depression.

The exact relationship between postpartum depression and breast-feeding is unclear. There have been several studies (1) indicating a relationship between breast-feeding for longer periods of time and a decreased incidence of postpartum depression. There are other studies, however, that indicate there is no protection against postpartum depression in women who breast-feed. Many of these studies, however, have been very small and have failed to control for confounding factors such as family income, marital status, social support, stressful life events, and maternal education.

There is some indication that depression in the mother may cause her to discontinue breast-feeding prematurity. In a large study, it was found that women who had depression and anxiety during the pregnancy were especially vulnerable to not only having postpartum depression but were more likely to discontinue breast-feeding early in the postpartum period. Unfortunately, in many of these women, the symptoms of postpartum depression often worsened after discontinuing breast-feeding.

Women who have the lowest risk of postpartum depression are those who have planned in advance to breast-feed and who are able to successfully nurse their infants. On the other hand, the highest risk of postpartum depression was found in women who had plans to breast-feed but did not carry out those plans after the birth of the baby. The risk of postpartum depression was also high in women who did not intend to breast-feed but ended up breast-feeding anyway.

Clinically, those women who do not plan to breast-feed are usually happy with their decision and have low rates of postpartum depression. Higher rates of postpartum depression are those women who, despite being committed to nursing their infants, are unable or who have difficulties with the breast-feeding process. The vulnerability to postpartum depression, therefore, seems to be related to having a breast-feeding outcome that differs from what the woman initially sets out to do.

Things that get in the way of breast-feeding, such as having a cesarean section, delivery complications, a baby with health issues, and difficulty breast-feeding, seem to impact the rate of postpartum depression in women who intended to breast-feed prior to the delivery of their baby.

Caring for the Breast-feeding Woman Who Is Depressed

Women who intend to breast-feed despite having postpartum depression need special attention. Things a caregiver must ask the woman include the following:

- How does the woman feel about taking an antidepressant while nursing her infant? Some women are reluctant to expose their infant to the effects of antidepressant medication and may be hesitant to take medications that could bring them out of their depression.
- Could it be possible that breast-feeding is contributing to the woman's sense of despair? Is breast-feeding not going as planned, or is she breast-feeding only out of obligation when she really does not like breast-feeding?
- Is the insistence on breast-feeding interfering with her being treated for postpartum depression? Again, she may be refusing medications because she fears they have a negative impact on the nursing infant.
- Does the woman have adequate guidance in order to wean off breast-feeding so that she doesn't otherwise aggravate the hormonal balance associated with breast-feeding? Hormones play a large role in postpartum depression, and stopping breast-feeding suddenly can negatively impact her psychological state.
- Does the woman have enough support and information to discontinue breast-feeding her infant, should that be the ultimate outcome? Stopping suddenly leads to physical and psychological outcomes that can lead to an increase in postpartum depressive symptoms.

In caring for the breast-feeding mother with postpartum depression, the health care provider must balance the benefits of breast-feeding the infant along with the theoretical risks of taking an antidepressant or another drug. The assessment of the situation must be case-specific.

The safest antidepressant possible should be used in the breast-feeding mother. If the woman has been on an antidepressant in the past that was successful, this should be the mediation attempted first. If the mother is on mediations, the pediatrician should be involved and should make every attempt to observe the infant for behavior indicating side effects of the medications.

Mothers should be advised to take their antidepressant at a time that minimizes the infant's exposure. This might mean taking the medication when the infant is likely to sleep the longest as the serum levels of the drug will be highest during that time.

If the mother is planning to wean off her antidepressant medication, she should do so slowly and should do it under medical supervision. Care must be taken to observe the mother for signs and symptoms of a relapse of her postpartum depression.

I thought, what if I cut the baby? Then I thought what kind of mother am I? I took out all the knives out of the kitchen and I wouldn't let any of the kids in the kitchen. What kind of woman am I?

—Postpartum woman

Dealing with Postpartum Emergencies

Caregivers should be aware of statements a new mother says that indicate she is at a greater risk of postpartum depression. Common statements a mother might say include the following:

- I have not slept at all in forty-eight hours or more.
- I do not feel loving toward my baby and can't even go through the motions of taking care of him or her.
- I am afraid I might harm myself in order to escape this pain.
- I am afraid I might do something to hurt the baby.
- I hear sounds or voices when no one is around.

- I feel that my thoughts are not my own or that they are totally out of my control.
- I have lost a lot of weight without trying to.
- I feel like such a bad mother.
- Maybe I should never have become a mother. I think I may have made a mistake.

If the pros and cons of breast-feeding while suffering from postpartum depression and taking medications have been explained to the mother and she decides to continue nursing her infant, she needs the support of her health care team as well as social support from her loved ones. She may need extra support from programs like La Leche League in order to adequately breast-feed her infant. She may also need extra support from health care providers specializing in breast-feeding and postpartum depression. Her partner needs to be involved in the decision to breast-feed while taking medications for postpartum depression.

Self-help options should be given to the mother whenever possible. This means that she should

- be encouraged to accept help from friends and family in caring for the infant and other children she may have.
- be encouraged to take more time for herself such as walking, taking a long bath, taking naps, and spending time alone with her spouse or partner.
- take time to discuss emotions with a caring and non-judgmental friend. If this is not possible, outpatient psychotherapy may help her deal with her emotions.
- be encouraged to refrain from being a perfectionist. Her expectations of motherhood should be realistic and flexible.
- be encouraged to nurture herself from a physical standpoint. This means that she rests as often as she can and sleeps when the infant is sleeping.
- be encouraged to eat a healthy diet and to take multivitamins. There is some evidence that vitamin B complex and omega-3 fatty acids from fish oil or from vegan sources can help improve mood and defend against depressive symptoms.
- be encouraged to express her anger safely. This can mean things like hitting a pillow, writing in a journal, or using exercise to disperse anger.
- Be encouraged to use her sense of humor. Laughing and keeping up a positive spirit can go a long way toward defense against depressive symptoms.

Women who are suffering from postpartum depression are usually able to continue breast-feeding and even take antidepressant medication if they are properly supervised and if the infant is followed carefully by the infant's pediatrician. If the woman recovers and decides to go off the medication, it should be done carefully and gradually so as to avoid a recurrence of postpartum depressive symptoms.

Tips for Antidepressant Medication Choices

Most antidepressants can be used in breast-feeding

SSRIs and most TCAs are considered safe with rare infant side effects reported such as reduced weight gain, increased crying, decreased sleep, gastrointestinal distress, and irritability.

About 5–9 percent of the mother's dose of fluoxetine (Prozac) is excreted in breast milk, and the infant's liver is less mature to handle long half-life, so it's not a first-line choice.

Overall, SSRIs do not increase the risk of autism spectrum disorder (ASD)

Some conflicting data shows that first-trimester exposure in boys has an increased risk of ASD.

Doxepin should not be used because of high concentrations of metabolites.

Nefazodone (Serzone) should be avoided if possible.

Long-term data shows no significant differences in neurobehavioral development in children of mothers who used antidepressants.

Tips for Antipsychotic Medication Choices

All are considered relatively safe in pregnancy

No major congenital malformation seen versus no medication treatment.

Most are Category C. Clozaril (Clozapine) and lurasidone (Latuda) are Class B.

Most second-generation antipsychotics are considered fairly safe. Avoid clozapine (Clozaril), iloperidone (Fanapt), and ziprasidone (Geodon).

Avoid loxapine, thioridazine, and thiothixene if possible.

Watch for transient abnormal muscle movements (EPS), seizures, respiratory distress, feeding difficulties, tachycardia, and low blood pressure in newborns.

First-generation antipsychotics (FGA) may cause EPS in the infant or other rare effects.

Atypical antipsychotics are preferred during pregnancy over classic mood stabilizers.

Tips for Mood Stabilizer Medication Choices

Lithium: Infant serum concentration up to 40 to 50 percent of mother's concentration.

Up to 30 percent of mother's lithium dose is excreted in breast milk. Breast-feeding is not recommended because of the risk of infant toxicity.

Low concentration in milk with valproic acid (Depakote), rare anemia and thrombocytopenia reported. If it's your only choice, keep doses less than 1000 mg per day and give folic acid.

Carbamazepine (Tegretol) has low concentrations in milk. Rare transient hepatic dysfunction has been reported.

The risks of using lamotrigine (Lamictal) during lactation are unknown.

Chapter 21

PSYCHIATRIC PHARMACOGENOMICS

I often tell women/clients two things when I meet them for the first time: first is that Freud is dead, and second is we can figure out what medications their body will tolerate to resolve their symptoms. I have used genetic testing (Assurex/GeneSight) in over four hundred patients and have found it to be an amazing tool to help individual their symptoms of mental illness. Previous portions of this book are about choosing medications for women during pregnancy, postpartum, and lactation and are clinical insights for empirical data. They will not tell you what an individual woman will respond to.

Psychiatrists and physicians have used empirical information to choose medications in the past. This is a rational trial-and-error system, titrating medications slowly to try to avoid side effects. This leads to a longer period of response time, and the patient is still symptomatic. Many of psychotropic medications carry black box warnings further complicating the choices for antidepressants, antipsychotics, and mood stabilizers. Studies have shown that clinicians augment with other medications often in an attempt to get a response sooner but has not been shown to be necessarily effective (226). Polypharmacy complicates the picture for pregnant and lactating women. Some individuals respond well to polypharmacy, while others are overmedicated by it.

Practicing physicians learn rapidly that different people respond to medications in different ways. A small individual may take large amounts of medication with no effect, while a large individual may be snowed by a very tiny dose. Often, we ask what another family member has responded to in an attempt to use this information to guide medication choices, which is really looking at their genetics.

Personalized medication management has been the goal of most physicians, but with the human genome sequencing, it is now possible to test using a buccal swab to learn what medications each individual will be able to respond to. This is true of all medications not just psychiatric medications and explains the drug-drug interactions that complicate medical management.

Genes used for clinical pharmacogenetics are broken down into two groups:

1) Pharmacokinetics (i.e., how much drug is in the system) – Polymorphisms in pharmacokinetic (PK) genes (e.g., CYP450) can affect drug blood levels.
2) Pharmacodynamics (i.e., how is the drug working when it gets to its target) –Polymorphisms in pharmacodynamics (PD) genes can affect drug action at its target (e.g. receptor binding).

Using different delivery mechanisms (e.g., IM, transdermal) does not compensate for variations in pharmacokinetic systems. While these mechanisms avoid first-pass metabolism, the medication will still eventually be metabolized in the liver.

Psychiatric pharmacogenomics testing delineates the cytochrome P450 gene. The CYP450 system is a family of about fifty-seven enzymes responsible for drug metabolism, primarily in the liver. Multiple enzymes may be involved in the metabolism of a given drug. Since most drugs are metabolized by multiple enzymes, a physician can't test for only one gene and expect a complete answer. Likewise, genetic variation in multiple pathways can also impact efficacy.

CYP2D6 is one of several important CYP450 genes that have common genetic polymorphisms. CYP2D6 is a gene where gene duplications can occur so individuals may have more than the normal two copies of the gene, which will impact how much medication will be available. These variations give multiple combinations that lead to different amounts of protein enzymes that will metabolize medications. There are a number of possible combinations of two alleles based on which alleles the parents possess. This can result in a wide range of liver function. To simplify matters, researchers have collapsed these genotypic realities into "buckets" based on the ultimate result on liver function. An individual with two normally functioning copies of CYP2D6 is known as an extensive metabolizer. (This is the normal response most medications are based on.)

A person that has one normal chromosome and one chromosome that contains three copies of CYP2D6 will result in twice the amount of CYP2D6 enzyme in the system, leading to an ultrarapid metabolizer phenotype.

Individuals with one "good" copy and one "bad" copy of a gene are considered "intermediate" metabolizers. These individuals retain CYP2D6 function, but at a reduced capacity. The individual has one normal copy and one gene deletion, resulting in 50 percent of the normal enzyme function. The individual may still be able to metabolize CYP2D6 substrates but may need lower doses. Drug-drug interactions are of greater concern in these individuals because of their already compromised metabolic capacity.

Poor metabolizers are individuals with little to no enzyme function. This can be the result of gene deletions or alleles that produce nonfunctional enzymes. These individuals will have significant problems metabolizing CYP2D6 substrates. Significant dose adjustments or alternative therapies are likely necessary.

Less than half of individuals are extensive metabolizers. A clinician can expect roughly 10 percent of his/her population to be poor metabolizers, and 10 percent will be ultrarapid metabolizers. This means that one in five (20 percent) of his/her population may be significantly impacted by their CYP2D6 status. And this is only one gene of many that is important for medication selection/dosing.

The FDA is well aware of the impact of genetic variation on medication selection and dosing. Yet very few clinicians have time to read the package inserts (PI) for the medications they prescribe. Twenty-nine of the thirty-eight medications on the psychotropic test have pharmacogenomics language in the PIs.

One example of a pharmacodynamics gene is the serotonin transporter. The serotonin transporter is the primary site of action for SSRIs as it is responsible for serotonin reuptake.

Serotonin Transporter (SLC6A4)

The serotonin transporter is encoded by the SLC6A4 gene. It is responsible for the reuptake of serotonin into the presynaptic neuron. Selective serotonin reuptake inhibitors (SSRIs) impede this process, allowing for more serotonin in the synaptic cleft.

The SLC6A4 promoter has two main variants: short (S) and long (L).The short allele results in lower transcription rates, providing less active sites for SSRIs. The short allele is associated with lower rates of remission following SSRI treatment.

The SLC6A4 promoter variant is one of the best studied genes in psychiatry. Multiple meta-analyses confirm significantly lower rates of response and remission in S/S and L/S individuals.

Serotonin transporter gene (SLC6A4), serotonin receptor 2A gene (HTR2A), and serotonin receptor 2C gene (HTR2C) explain if individuals will respond to serotonin reuptake inhibitors, such as fluoxetine (Prozac), sertraline (Zoloft), paroxetine (Paxil), citalopram (Celexa), and escitalopram (Lexapro).

The promoter region is the "on/off switch" of the gene. It tells the gene to transcribe more or less mRNA. The 44bp deletion causes lower transcription rates, resulting in fewer transporters on the presynaptic neuron. This genotype is associated with lower response rate.

MTHFR

Folate is necessary for the formation of the neural development of the fetus. Folate also plays a critical role in the formation of SAMe, an important precursor to neurotransmitter synthesis.1

Folic acid (synthetic form) and dihydrofolate (dietary form) must be converted to l-methyl folate, the usable form, by methylenetetrahydrofolate reductase, an enzyme encoded by the MTHFR gene.2 The methyl folate is necessary to cross the blood-brain barrier and the placenta to become the precursor for neurotransmitter synthesis. Pharmacogenetics will tell if the individual has a genetic mutation and needs folate supplementation with l-methyl folate (5-MTHF), the active form of folate.

Several recent studies have shown that increasing the intake of folic acid can overcome the effect of reduced MTHFR activity, although this has the potential to mask a vitamin B12 deficiency.

I also tell individuals that psychiatric pharmacogenomics has brought psychiatric treatment out of the dark ages. It no longer has to be just trial and error, which patients describe as being a lab rat. Medication management can now be a shared process rather than the doctor not listening to their concerns about medication.

Although pharmacogenomics is a relatively new science and will no doubt be refined in the coming years, in this author's opinion, current genetic testing provides a platform for which clinicians can make their best attempt to personalize medication selection.

Chapter 22

CONCLUSION

Pregnancy and the postpartum period are supposed to be times of joy and happiness. Unfortunately, some women enter these states already suffering from a mental illness, such as depression, anxiety, and psychotic illness. They face the difficulties in deciding whether or not to stop taking the medications they have been on before being pregnant, facing the chance of relapse.

Other women have had a history of mental illness in the past or have never had a mental illness but develop symptoms while they are pregnant or breast-feeding. They too face decisions on what to do about their symptoms, knowing that all medications taken in pregnancy expose the fetus to these same medications.

Research has shown that not treating the mental illness can be just as dangerous as taking medications for the disorder. Women who are mentally ill in pregnancy tend not to receive adequate antepartum care and can have pregnancy complications such as prematurity, infant death, and preeclampsia. Women who develop postpartum depression or postpartum psychosis can be dangerous to themselves or to those around them. While women with postpartum depression or postpartum psychosis rarely harm their babies, they are at risk of harming themselves, committing suicide, and disrupting the mother-infant bond in ways that can negatively affect the infant's outcome.

All psychotropic drugs will cross the placental barrier during the time of in utero development and have the possibility of causing overt birth defects or subtle changes in the neural development of the infant. Unfortunately, there are few studies on the use of psychotropic medications in pregnancy and breast-feeding because no researcher wants to intentionally expose an infant to a potentially harmful drug during pregnancy or breast-feeding. Instead, studies have been done on women who took the drug and didn't know they were pregnant or who chose to take the medication despite being pregnant.

Most of the time, the birth defect rate in pregnancy did not increase the baseline rate of birth defects found in women who were unexposed to the drug. There are a few drugs that have shown trends in birth defects that should be avoided in pregnancy, especially during the first trimester when the major organs are being developed.

Taking psychotropic medications has been associated in some situations with neonatal withdrawal syndrome, in which the infant, exposed in the third trimester, develops poor feeding, tremulousness, and other symptoms because of withdrawal from the drug. Most of the time, these symptoms are self-limited and go away in a few days without intervention. Rarely is an infant truly addicted to a drug given in pregnancy, with the exception of certain illicit drugs such as opioid medications. In such cases, the infant may have to be tapered off the opioid drug gradually over time to avoid the brunt of withdrawal symptoms.

After the delivery of the baby, many women can suffer a relapse of their mental illness or can develop a new onset of a mental illness such as postpartum depression or postpartum psychosis. For these women, there are screening tools such as the Beck Depression Inventory or the Edinburgh Postnatal Depression Scale (EPDS) that are usually given to the woman on the first postnatal visit. Such screening tools have been found to be invaluable in identifying high-risk women who go on for further psychiatric evaluation and treatment.

Fortunately, some women respond to nonpharmacologic therapy such as cognitive behavioral therapy and family-based therapy, which can help a woman cope with her symptoms without having to worry about taking medications and the complications that might go with it. Others can undergo electroconvulsive therapy (ECT), which can provide relief of depression and psychotic symptoms without harming the mother or fetus.

In other cases, no amount of psychotherapy or ECT can control the symptoms, and medications are offered to the woman along with the above modalities. This becomes a risk-benefit decision that must be made with the available data on the risk of taking the medications versus the risk of not treating the illness in the pregnant or breast-feeding mother. While this is compounded by the fact that few studies are out there, some determination can be made on past case histories and small studies on the effects of the medication on the fetus at different points during the pregnancy.

Pregnancy and the postpartum state are not protective against mental illness and, in fact, are stressors that can precipitate stress and mental illness in many women. The rate of postpartum depression alone is 10–20 percent—plenty of women to make it somewhat of an epidemic among women of child-rearing age. Because these mental illnesses are so prevalent, more research is necessary to determine whether there are any long-term consequences to the fetus or newborn exposed to the various psychotropic medications available.

Resources

There are resources for providers and mothers dealing with postpartum depression and who have decided to breast-feed. These include the following:

- Perinatal Depression Project at the University of Illinois in Chicago. This is a provider consultation line for physicians to get advice on how to manage a postpartum woman who is breast-feeding and dealing with PPD. The number is 1-800-573-6121.
- MedEdPPD.org. This is a site at the National Institute of Mental Health that can be accessed by anyone interested in PPD and breast-feeding.
- Breast-feeding Pharmacology. This is provided by Dr. Thomas Hale and can be accessed online by typing www.neonatal.ttuhsc.edu/lact.
- Emory Women's Mental Health Program through the Emory University in Atlanta, Georgia (womensmentalhealth.emory.edu)
- Local breast-feeding support groups at local hospitals or through the La Leche League
- The Infant Risk Center (infantrisk.com) – It is dedicated to providing evidence-based information about medications during pregnancy and lactation. Call 1-806-352-2519.
- LactMed app – It is available from the US National Library of Medicine at the National Institute of Health. This app provides information about drugs and chemicals, listing any possible adverse effects for nursing an infant with suggestions of safe alternatives.
- Nan Nelson, MD
- nanenelsonmd@gmail.com
- 330-557-0586
- Spectrum Health
- 616-391-1771
- 616-391-5000
- nancy.roberts@spectrum-health.org
- National Pregnancy Registration for Psychiatric Medications
- 1-866-961-2388
- http://womensmentalhealth.org/clinical-and-research-programs/pregnancyregistry
- Motherisk (Motherisk is in Canada and is an amazing resource)
- http://www.motherisk.org/women/drugs.isp
- Australian Perinatal Psychotropic Medicines Information Service (PPMIS)
- http://www.ppmis.org.au/
- Canadian Center for Addiction and Mental Health

- http://www.camhx.ca/Publications/Resources for Professionals/ Pregnancy Lactation/psychmedpreglact.pdf

Screening and Rating Scales

Edinburgh Postnatal Depression Scale
"As you are pregnant or have recently had a baby, we would like to know how you are feeling. Please check the answer that comes closest to how you have felt in the past seven days, not just how you feel today."

1. I have been able to laugh and see the funny side of things.
   o As much as I always could
   o Not quite as much now
   o Definitely not so much now
   o I haven't been coping as well at all

2. I have looked forward with enjoyment to things.
   o As much as I ever did
   o Rather less than I used to
   o Definitely less than I used to
   o Hardly at all

3. I have blamed myself unnecessarily when things went wrong.
   o Yes, most of the time
   o Yes, some of the time
   o Not very often
   o No, never

4. I have been anxious or worried for no good reason.
   o No, not at all
   o Hardly ever
   o Yes, some of the time
   o Yes, very often

5. I have felt scared or panicky for no very good reason.
   o Yes, quite a bit
   o Yes, sometimes
   o No, not much
   o No, not at all

6. Things have been getting on top of me.

o   Yes, most of the time I haven't been able to cope at all
o   Yes, sometimes I haven't been able to cope as usual
o   No, most of the time I have coped quite well
o   No, I have been coping as well as ever

7.   I have been so unhappy that I have had difficulty sleeping.
o   Yes, most of the time
o   Yes, sometimes
o   Not very often
o   No, not at all

8.   I have felt sad or miserable.
o   Yes, most of the time
o   Yes, quit often
o   No, not very often
o   No, not at all

9.   I have been so unhappy that I have been crying.
o   Yes, most of the time
o   Yes, quite often
o   Only occasionally
o   No, never

10. The thought of harming myself has occurred to me.
o   Yes, quite often
o   Sometimes
o   Hardly ever
o   Never

Scoring:

For questions 1, 2, and 4, these are scored as 0, 1, 2, or 3, with the top box scored as 3. For questions 3 and 5–10, they are scored reversed, with the top box scored as 3 and the bottom box scored as 0.

The maximum score is 30 possible points. There is an indication of possible depression with a score of 10 or greater. Pay special attention to question 10 as it relates to suicidal ideation.

Women who score greater than 10 on the scale are referred to a mental health specialist to see if she has postpartum depression and for treatment, if indicated.

The Beck Depression Inventory

Some obstetricians and psychiatrists prefer the Beck Depression Inventory, which is a general screening tool for the detection of depression. It is a 21-point questionnaire that is self-taken and self-scored. The Beck Depression Inventory goes as follows:

1.
0   I do not feel sad.
1   I feel sad.
2   I am sad all the time and I can't snap out of it.
3   I am so sad and unhappy that I can't stand it.

2.
0   I am not particularly discouraged about the future.
1   I feel discouraged about the future.
2   I feel I have nothing to look forward to.
3   I feel the future is hopeless and that things cannot improve.

3.
0   I do not feel like a failure.
1   I feel I have failed more than the average person.
2   As I look back on my life, all I can see is a lot of failures.
3   I am a complete failure as a person.

4.
0   I get as much satisfaction out of things as I used to.
1   I don't enjoy things the way I used to.
2   I don't get real satisfaction out of anything anymore.
3   I am dissatisfied or bored with everything.

5.
0   I don't feel particularly guilty.
1   I feel guilty a good part of the time.
2   I feel quite guilty most of the time.
3   I feel guilty all of the time.

6.
0   I don't feel I am being punished.
1   I feel I may be punished.
2   I expect to be punished.

3   I feel I am being punished.

7.

0   I don't feel disappointed in myself.
1   I am disappointed in myself.
2   I am disgusted with myself.
3   I hate myself.

8.

0   I don't feel I am any worse than anybody else.
1   I am critical of myself for my weaknesses or mistakes.
2   I blame myself all the time for my faults.
3   I blame myself for everything bad that happens.

9.

0   I don't have any thoughts of killing myself.
1   I have thoughts of killing myself but would not carry them out.
2   I would like to kill myself.
3   I would kill myself if I had the chance.

10.

0   I don't cry any more than usual.
1   I cry more now than I used to.
2   I cry all the time now.
3   I used to be able to cry, but now I can't cry even though I want to.

11.

0   I am no more irritated by things than I ever was.
1   I am slightly more irritated now than usual.
2   I am quite annoyed or irritated a good deal of the time.
3   I feel irritated all of the time.

12.

0   I have not lost interest in other people.
1   I am less interested in other people than I used to be.
2   I have lost most of my interest in other people.
3   I have lost all of my interest in other people.

13.

0   I make decisions about a well as I ever could.
1   I put off making decisions more than I used to.
2   I have greater difficulty in making decisions more than I used to.

3   I can't make decisions at all anymore.

14.

0   I don't feel that I look any worse than I used to.

1   I am worried that I am looking old or unattractive.

2   I feel there are permanent changes in my appearance that make me look unattractive.

3   I believe that I look ugly.

15.

0   I can work about as well as before.

1   It takes an extra effort to get started at doing something.

2   I have to push myself very hard to do anything.

3   I can't do any work at all.

16.

0   I can sleep as well as usual.

1   I don't sleep as well as I used to.

2   I wake up several hours earlier than I used to and find it hard to get back to sleep.

3   I wake up several hours earlier than I used to and cannot get back to sleep.

17.

0   I don't get more tired than usual.

1   I get tired more easily than I used to.

2   I get tired from doing almost anything.

3   I am too tired to do anything.

18.

0   My appetite is no worse than usual.

1   My appetite is not as good as it used to be.

2   My appetite is much worse now.

3   I have no appetite at all anymore.

19.

0   I haven't lost much weight, if any, lately.

1   I have lost more than 5 pounds.

2   I have lost more than 10 pounds.

3   I have lost more than 15 pounds.

20.

0   I am not worried about my health than usual.

1   I am worried about physical problems like aches, pains, or upset stomach.
2   I am very worried about physical problems and it is hard to think of much else.
3   I am so worried about my physical problems that I cannot think of anything else.

21.
0   I have not noticed any recent change in my interest in sex.
1   I am less interested in sex than I used to be.
2   I have almost no interest in sex.
3   I have lost interest in sex completely.

Interpreting the Beck Depression Inventory

Now that you have completed the questionnaire, add up the score for each of the twenty-one questions by counting the number to the right of each question you marked. The highest-possible total for the whole test would be sixty-three. This would mean that you circled 3 on all twenty-one questions. Since the lowest possible score for each question is zero, the lowest-possible score would be zero. This would mean you circled 0 on each question. You can evaluate your depression according to the table below:

Total Score: _____

Levels of Depression: 1–10 These ups and downs are considered normal
11–16 Mild mood disturbance
17–20 Borderline clinical depression
21–30 Moderate depression
31–40 Severe depression
Over 40 indicates extreme depression

If you have a consistent score of seventeen or more, you may need some medical or psychiatric depression.

Of the two tests, the Edinburgh Postnatal Depression Score is considered the preferable test for women at risk for postnatal depression and can be given over the phone or in person to the postpartum mother. The Beck Depression Inventory includes sleep and appetite questions as well as weight changes that are a natural part of childbirth and therefore does not give a complete picture.

The Mood Disorder Questionnaire (195)

The Mood Disorder Questionnaire is a "yes-no" questionnaire that includes the following:

1. Has there ever been a period of time when you were not your usual self and

   - you felt so good or hyper that other people thought you were not your normal self, or you were so hyper that you got into trouble?
   - you were so irritable that you shouted at people or started fights or arguments?
   - you felt more self-confident than usual?
   - you got much less sleep than usual and found you didn't really miss it?
   - you were much more talkative or spoke much faster than usual?
   - you had thoughts racing through your mind or couldn't slow your mind down?
   - you were so easily distracted by things around you that you had trouble concentrating or staying on track?
   - you had much more energy than usual?
   - you were much more active or did many more things than usual?
   - you were much more social or outgoing than usual, such as telephoning your friends in the middle of the night?
   - you were much more interested in sex than usual?
   - you did things that were unusual for you or that other people might have thought were excessive, foolish, or risky?
   - you spent money that got you or a family into trouble?

2. If you answered *yes* to more than one of the above, have several of these ever happened during the same period of time?
3. How much of a problem did any of these cause you, such as being unable to work; having family, money, or legal troubles; and getting into arguments or fights?
4. Have any of your blood relatives had manic depressive illness or bipolar disorder?
5. Has a health professional ever told you that you have manic depressive illness or bipolar disorder?

If the patient answered *yes* to seven or more of the items under question 1 and *yes* to question 2 and answered "moderate" or "serious" to question 3, this represents a positive screen for a bipolar mood disorder. All three of the above criteria should be positive for the disorder.

The DASS-21 Scale is as follows:

Over the past week,
1. I found it hard to wind down.
2. I was aware of dryness in my mouth.
3. I couldn't seem to experience any positive feelings at all.
4. I experienced breathing difficulty.
5. I found it difficult to work up the initiative to do things.
6. I tended to overreact to situations.
7. I experienced trembling.
8. I felt that I was using a lot of nervous energy.
9. I was worried about situations in which I might panic or make a fool of myself.
10. I felt that I had nothing to look forward to.
11. I found myself getting agitated.
12. I found it difficult to relax.
13. I felt downhearted and blue.
14. I was intolerant of anything that kept me from getting on with what I was doing.
15. I was close to panic.
16. I was unable to be enthusiastic about doing anything.
17. I felt I wasn't worth much as a person.
18. I felt that I was rather touchy.
19. I was aware of the action of my heart in the absence of physical exertion.
20. I felt scared without any good reason.
21. I felt that life was meaningless.

Women answered whether they felt these things not at all, some of the time, a good part of the time, or most of the time. There are items on the DASS-21 that are directly related to increased stress.

The DASS-21 has been found to distinguish reliably between the symptoms of depression, anxiety, and stress in nonclinical and clinical samples (178). The researchers recommend that the DASS-21 be used along with clinical interviews in order to identify anxiety and depression in the postpartum state.

References

111A

1. Flynn HA, et al. "Rates and predictors of depression treatment among pregnant women in hospital-affiliated obstetrics practices. General Hospital Psychiatry. July–Aug 2006. Vol 28, No 4; pp 289–929.

2. Kendell RE, et al. "Psychiatric hospitalizations for women during perinatal years." Br J Psychiatry. 1987. Vol 150; pp 662–673.

3. Cohen LS, et al. "Relapse of major depression during pregnancy in women who maintain or discontinue antidepressant treatment." JAMA. 2006. Vol 295, No 5; pp 499–507.

4. Evans J, et al. "Cohort study of depressed mood during pregnancy and after childbirth." BMJ. 2001. 323; pp 257–260.

5. http://www.drugs.com/pregnancy-categories.html. Accessed 12/6/2015.

6. Einarson TR, Einarson A. "Newer antidepressants in pregnancy and rates of major malformations: a meta-analysis of prospective comparative studies." Pharmacoepidemiol Drug Saf. 2005. Vol 14, No 12; pp 823–827.

7. Chun-Fai-Chan B, Koren G, et al. "Pregnancy outcome of women exposed to bupropion during pregnancy: a prospective comparative study." March 2005. Vol 192, No 3.

8. Cole JA, Modell JG, et al. "Bupropion in pregnancy and the prevalence of congenital malformations." Pharmacoepidemiol Drug Saf. 9 August 2006.

9. Levinson-Castiel R, Merlob P, Linder N, Sirota L, Klinger G. "Neonatal abstinence syndrome after in utero exposure to selective serotonin reuptake inhibitors in term infants." Arch Pediatr Adolesc Med. 2006 Feb. Vol 160, No 2; pp 173–6.

10. Laine K, Heikkinen T, Ekblad U, Kero P." Effects of exposure to selective serotonin reuptake inhibitors during pregnancy on serotonergic symptoms in newborns and cord blood monoamine and prolactin concentrations." Arch Gen Psychiatry. 2003 Jul. Vol 60, No 7; pp 720–6.

2.11.   Misri S, Oberlander TF, Fairbrother N, Carter N, Ryan D, Kuan AJ, Reebye P. "Relation between prenatal maternal mood and anxiety and neonatal health." Can J Psychiatry. 2004 Oct; Vol 49.

3.12.   Misri S, Oberlander TF, Fairbrother N, Carter N, Ryan D, Kuan AJ, Reebye P. "Relation between prenatal maternal mood and anxiety and neonatal health." Can J Psychiatry. 2004 Oct. Vol 49, No 10; pp 684–9.

13. Nulman I, Rovet J, Stewart DE, Wolpin J, Pace-Asciak P, Shuhaiber S, Koren G. "Child development following exposure to tricyclic antidepressants or fluoxetine throughout fetal life: a prospective, controlled study." Am J Psychiatry. 2002 Nov. Vol 159, No 11; pp 1889–95.

14. Chambers CD, Hernandez-Diaz S, et al. "Selective serotonin-reuptake inhibitors and risk of persistent pulmonary hypertension of the newborn." New England Journal of Medicine 2006; No 354, Vol 6; pp 579–87.

4.15.   Nulman I, et al. "Neurodevelopment of children exposed in utero to antidepressant drugs." N Engl J Med. 1997. Jan 23. Vol 336, No 4; pp 258–62.

16. Payne, JL. "Antidepressant use in the postpartum period: practical considerations." American Journal of Psychiatry. 2007. Vol 164, No 9; pp 1329–32.

5.17.Meador KJ, Baker GA, et al. NEAD Study Group. "Cognitive function at 3 years of age after fetal exposure to antiepileptic drugs." N Engl J Med. 2009 Apr 16. Vol 360, No 16; pp 1597–605.

18. Cooper WO, Point ME, Ray WA. "Increasing use of antidepressants in pregnancy." Am J Obstet Gynecol. 2007. Vol 196; pp 544 el.

19. Field T, et al. "Prenatal depression effects on the fetus and newborn: a review." Infant Behav Dev. 2006. Vol 29; pp 445–55.

20. Kallen BA, et al. "Maternal use of selective serotonin reuptake inhibitors in early pregnancy and infant congenital malformations." Birth Defects Res a Clin Mol Teratol.

6.21.   Hemels M, et al. "Antidepressant use during pregnancy and the rates of spontaneous abortions: a meta-analysis." Ann Pharmacother. 2005. Vol 19. https://womensmentalhealth.org/clinical-and-research-

7.22.   Oberlander T, et al. "Effects of timing and duration of gestational exposure to serotonin reuptake inhibitors: population based study." Br J Psychiatry. 2008. Vol 192; pp 338–43.

23. Simon G, et al. "Outcomes of prenatal antidepressant exposure." Am J Psychiatry. 2002. Vol 159; pp 2055–61.

24. Cole J, et al. "Buproprion in pregnancy and the prevalence of congenital malformations." Pharmacoepidemiol Drug Saf. 2007. Vol 16; pp 474–84.

8.25.   Costei A, et al. "Perinatal outcome following third trimester exposure to paroxetine." Arch Pediatr Adolesc Med. 2002. Vol 156; pp 1129–32.

26. Nulman I, et al. "Neurodevelopment of children exposed in utero to antidepressant drugs." New Engl J Med. 1997. Vol 336; pp 258–62.

27. Wisner K, et al. "Pharmacological treatment of depression during pregnancy." JAMA. 1999. Vol 282; pp 1264–9.

9.28. Wisner K, et al. "Tricyclic dose requirements across pregnancy." Am J Psychiatry. 1993. Vol 150, No 10; pp 1541–2.

29. Cohen LS, et al. "Relapse of major depression during pregnancy in women who maintain or discontinue antidepressant treatment. JAMA. 2006. Vol 295, No 5; 499–507.

10.30. Villeponteux VA, et al. "The effects of pregnancy on preexisting panic disorder." J Clin Psychiatry. 1992. Vol 53; pp 201–203

11.31. https://womensmentalhealth.org/clinical-and-research-programs/pregnancyregistry/?doing_wp_cron=1449444383.2303979396820068359375. Accessed 12/7/2015.

32. FDA Drug Safety Communication. Antipsychotic drug labels updated on use during pregnancy and risk of abnormal muscle movements and withdrawal symptoms in newborns.

33. U.S. Department of Health and Human Services. https://www.womenshealth.gov/. Accessed 12/7/2015.

34. Weinstock M. "Alterations induced by gestational stress in brain morphology and behavior of the offspring." Progress in Neurobiology. 2001; 65; pp 427–451.

35. Schneider M, Moore CF, et al. "Prenatal stress alters early neurobehavior, stress reactivity and learning in non-human primates: a brief review." Stress. Vol 4; pp 183–193.

36. Hansen D, et al. "Serious life events and congenital malformations: a national study with complete follow up." Lancet. 2000. Vol 356; pp 875–880.

37. Hedegaard, et al. "Psychological distress in pregnancy and preterm delivery. BMJ. 1993. Vol 307; pp 235–239.

38. Lou HC, Nordentoft M, et al. "Psychological stress and severe prematurity." Lancet. Vol 340; pp 54.

39. O'Connor, et al. "Maternal antenatal anxiety and children's behavioral/emotional problems at 4 years. Report from the Avalon Longitudinal Study of Parents and Children." British Journal of Psychiatry. 2002.

40. Hultman CM, et al. "Prenatal and perinatal risk factors for schizophrenia, affective psychosis, and reactive psychosis of early onset: case-control study." BMJ. 1999. Vol. 318; pp 421–426.

12.41. Gitau R, Fisk N, Teixeira J, et al. "Fetal HPA stress responses to invasive procedures are independent of maternal responses." Journal of Clinical and Endocrinological Metabolism. 2001. Vol 86; pp 104–109.

42. Kurki T, Hilesmaa V, et al. "Depression and anxiety in early pregnancy and risk for preeclampsia." Obstetrics and Gynecology. April 2000. Vol 95; (4); pp 487–490.

43. Smeenk JMJ, et al. "The effect of anxiety and depression on the outcome of in-vitro fertilization." Human Reproduction. 2001. Vol 15; pp 1420–1423.

44. Mahlstedt PP. "The psychological component of infertility." Fertil Steril. 1985. Vol 43; pp 335–346.

45. Boivin J, Takefman J. "Stress levels across stages of in vitro fertilization in subsequently pregnant and nonpregnant women." Fertil Steril. 1995. Vol 64; pp 802–810.

46. http://www.tommys.org/pregnancy/health/mental-health/anxiety-and-panic-attacks. Accessed 12/11/2015.

26. Kurki T, Hilesmaa V, et al. "Depression and anxiety in early pregnancy and risk for preeclampsia." Obstetrics and Gynecology. April 2000. Vol 95; (4); pp 487–490.

27. http://www.babycenter.com/0_managing-stress-and-anxiety-during-pregnancy_1683.bc. Accessed 12/11/2015.

28. Russell EJ, Fawcett JM, Mazmanian D. "OCD and pregnancy." Journal of Clinical Psychology. 2013. Vol 74, No 4; pp 377–385.

29. http://www.cfp.ca/content/60/2/133.full. Accessed 12/11/2015.

30. http://www.nimh.nih.gov/health/topics/bipolar-disorder/index.shtml. Accessed 12/11/2015.

31. Newport DJ, et al. "Lithium placental passage and obstetrical outcome: implications for clinical management during late pregnancy." Am J Psychiatry. 2005. Vol 162; pp 2162–2170.

32. Morrow J, Russell A, Guthrie E, et al. "Malformation risks of antiepileptic drugs in pregnancy: a prospective study from the UK Epilepsy and Pregnancy Register." J Neurol Neurosurg Psychiatr. 2006. Vol 77; pp 193–198.

33. Jager-Roman E. "Fetal growth, major malformations, and minor anomalies in infants born to women receiving valproic acid." J Pediatrics. 1986. Vol 108; pp 997–1004.

34. McKenna K, et al. "Pregnancy outcome of women using atypical antipsychotic drugs: a prospective comparative study." J Clin Psychiatry. 2005. Vol 66; pp 444–449.

35. Impastato D, et al. "Electric and insulin shock therapy during pregnancy." Dis Nerv Syst. 1964. Vol 25; pp 542–546.

36. Patton SW, et al. "Antipsychotic medications during pregnancy and lactation in women with schizophrenia: evaluating the risk." Can J Psychiatry. 2002. Vol 47; pp 959–965.

37. Santvana S, et al. "Psychiatric disorders associated with pregnancy." J Obstet Gynecol India. May/June 2005. Vol 55, No 3; pp 218–227.

38. http://www.nhs.uk/Conditions/Psychosis/Pages/Symptoms.aspx. Accessed 12/12/2015.

39. Goodman SH, Emory EK. "Perinatal complications in births to low socio-economic status schizophrenic and depressed women." Journal of Abnormal Psychology. 1992. Vol 101; pp 225–229.

40. Lis Y, Mann RD. "The Vamp research multi-purpose database in the UK." Journal of Clinical Epidemiology. 1995. Vol 48; pp 41–43.

41. Substance Abuse and Mental Health Services Administration. Results from the 2010 National Survey on Drug Use and Health: summary of national findings. NSDUH Series H-41, HHS Publication No. (SMA) 11-4658. Rockville (MD): SAHMSA; 2011.

42. Azadi A, Dildy GA. "Universal screening for substance abuse at the time of parturition." Am J Obstet Gynecol. 2008. Vol 198; pp e30–32.

43. Katenbach K, Berghella V, Finnegan L. "Opioid dependence during pregnancy. Effects and management." Obstet Gynecol Clin North Am. 1998. Vol 25; pp 138–151.

44. Bracken MB, Holford TR. "Exposure to prescribed drugs in pregnancy and association with congenital malformations." Obstet Gynecol. 1981. Vol 58; pp 336–44.

45. Substance abuse reporting and pregnancy: the role of the obstetrician-gynecologists. Committee Opinion No. 473. American College of Obstetricians and Gynecologists. Obstet Gynecol. 2011. Vol 117; pp 200–1.

46. Ewing H. A practical guide to intervention in health and social services with pregnant and postpartum addicts and alcoholics: theoretical framework, brief screening tool, key interview questions, and strategies for referral to recovery resources. Martinez (CA): The Born Free Project, Contra Costa County Department of Health Services; 1990.

47. Center for Adolescent Substance Abuse Research, Children's Hospital Boston. The CRAFFT screening interview. Boston (MA): CeASAR; 2009.

48. Center for Substance Abuse Treatment. Medication-assisted treatment for opioid addiction during pregnancy. In: SAHMSA/CSAT treatment improvement protocols. Rockville (MD): Substance Abuse and Mental Health Services Administration; 2008.

49. Cleary BJ, et al. "Methadone dose and neonatal abstinence syndrome—systemic review and meta-analysis." Addiction. 2010. Vol 105; pp 2071–84.

50. Institute of Medicine. Federal regulation of methadone treatment. Washington DC: National Academy Press; 1995.

51. Johnson RE, Jones HE, Fisher G. "The use of buprenorphine in pregnancy: patient management and effects on the neonate." Drug Alcohol Depend. 2003. Vol 70; pp 587–101.

52. Jones HE, et al. "Neonatal abstinence syndrome after methadone or buprenorphine exposure." N Engl J Med. 2010. Vol 363; pp 2320–31.

53. Meyer M, et al. "Intrapartum and postpartum analgesia for women maintained on methadone during pregnancy." Obstet Gynecol. 2007. Vol 110; pp 261–6.

54. Jones HE, Johnson RE, Milio L. "Post-cesarean pain management of patients maintained on methadone or buprenorphine." Am J Addict. 2006. Vol 15; pp 258–9.

55. Jones HE, Johnson RE, O'Grady KE, et al. "Dosing adjustments in postpartum patients maintained on buprenorphine or methadone." J Addict Med. 2008. Vol 2; pp 103–7.

56. Johnson RE, Jones HE, Fischer C. "Use of buprenorphine in pregnancy: patient management and effects on the neonate." Drug Alcohol Depend. 2003. Vol 70; pp 587–101.

26.57. Kaltenbach K, Finnegan LP. "Developmental outcome of children born to methadone maintained women: a review of longitudinal studies." Neurobehav Toxicol Teratol. 1984. Vol 6; pp 271–5.

27.58. Cox JL, Holden JM, and Sagovsky R. "Detection of postnatal depression: development of the 10-item Edinburgh Postnatal Depression Scale." British Journal of Psychiatry. 1987. Vol 150; pp 782–786.

28.59. 63 Wisner KL, Parry BL, Piontek CM. "Postpartum depression." N Engl J Med. 2002. Vol 347 (3); pp 194–199.

29.60. Beck AT. "Psychometric Properties of the Beck Depression Inventory." Clinical Psychiatric Review. 1988. Vol 8, No 1; pp 77–100.

61. American Psychiatric Association. (2013). Diagnostic and statistical manual of mental disorders: DSM-IV-TR (4th ed. text rev.). Washington, DC: American Psychiatric Association.

62. McFarlane AC. "The long-term costs of traumatic stress: intertwined physical and psychological consequences." World Psychiatry. 2010. Vol 9, No 1; pp 3–10.

63. Edhborg M, Matthiesen AS, et al. "Some early indicators for depressive symptoms and bonding two months postpartum: a study of new mothers and fathers. Archives of Women's Mental Health. 2005. Vol 8; pp 221–31.

64. Clark R, Tluczek A, Brown R. "A mother-infant therapy group model for postpartum depression." Infant Mental Health Journal. 2008. Vol 29; pp 514–36.

65. Joy S, Contag SA, Templeton HB. Postpartum Depression. E-medicine from WebMD. 2010. emedicine.medscape.com/article/271662-overview (accessed 12/12/21015).

66. Campbell SB, Cohn IF, Meyers T. "Depression in first time mothers; mother-infant interaction and depression chronicity. Developmental Psychology. 1995. Vol 31; pp 349–57.

67. Egeland B, Weinfield NS, Bosquet M, Cheng VK. Remembering, repeating, and working through: lessons from attachment-based interventions. Osofsky JD, Fitzgerald HE (eds). WAIMH Handbook of Infant Mental Health: infant mental health in groups at high risk (4e) New York: John Wiley and Sons, 2000, pp 35–89.

68. Jones NA, et al. "EEG during different emotions in ten-month-old infants of depressed mothers." Journal of Reproductive and Infant Psychology. 2001. Vol 19; pp 295–312.

69. Feldman R. "Parent-infant synchrony and the construction of shared timing: physiological precursors, developmental outcomes and risk conditions." Journal of Child Psychology and Psychiatry. 2007. Vol 48; pp 329–54.

70. Nagata M, Nagai Y, et al. "Maternity blues and attachment to children in mothers of full-term normal infants." Acta Psychiatrica Scandinavica. 2000. Vol 101; pp 209–17.

71. Cohn JF, et al. "Face to face interactions of postpartum depressed and non-depressed mother-infant pairs at two months." Developmental Psychology. 1990. Vol 26; pp 15–23.

72. Rutter M. "Psychiatric disorder in parents as a risk factor for children." In: SchaVer D, Philips I, NB Enger NB, eds. Prevention of mental disorder, alcohol and other drug use in children and adolescents. Rockville, Maryland: OYce for Substance Abuse, USDHHS, 1989.

73. Lyons-Ruth K, et al. "The depressed mother and her one year old infant: environment, interaction, attachment and infant development." In: Tronick EZ, Field T, eds. Maternal depression and infant disturbance. New directions for child development. San Francisco: JosseyBass, 1986.

74. Murray L. "The impact of postnatal depression on infant development." J Child Psychol Psychiatry. 1992. Vol 33; pp 543–6.

75. Campbell SB, Cohn JF, Meyers T. "Depression in first time mothers: mother-infant interaction and depression chronicity." Developmental Psychology. 1995. Vol 31; pp 349–57.

76. Weissman MM, Paykel ES. The depressed woman: a study of social relationships. Chicago: University of Chicago Press, 1974.

77. Cohn JF, Matias R, et al. "Face to face interaction of depressed mothers and their infants." In, Tronick EZ, Field T, eds. Maternal depression and infant disturbance. New directions for child development. San Francisco: Jossey-Bass, 1986; pp 34.

78. Cooper PJ, Murray L. "Prediction, detection, and treatment of postnatal depression. Arch Dis Child. 1997. Vol 77; pp 97–9.

79. Teti DM, Gefland DM, et al. "Depressed mother's behavioral competence with their infants: demographic and psychosocial correlates." Developmental and Psychopathology. 1990. Vol 2; pp 259–70.

80. Roberts, Nancy. Supporting Breastfeeding Mothers through Postpartum Depression. March 2004.

81. Cooper PJ, Murray L. "The impact of psychological treatments of postpartum depression on maternal mood and infant development." In, Murry L, Cooper PJ, eds. Postpartum Depression and Child Development. New York: Guilford Press, 1997. pp 201–20.

82. Nylen KJ, Moran TE, et al. "Maternal depression: a review of relevant treatment approaches for mothers and infants." Infant Mental Health Journal. 2006. Vol 27; pp 327–43.

83. Clark R, Thuczek A, Wenzel A. "Psychotherapy for postpartum depression: a preliminary report." American Journal of Orthopsychiatry. 2003. Vol 73; pp 441–54.

84. Poobalan AS, Aucott LS, et al. "Effects of treating postnatal depression on the mother-infant interaction and child development." British Journal of Psychiatry. 2007. Vol 191; pp 378–86.

85. Nylen KJ, Moran TE, et al. "Maternal depression: a review of relevant treatment approaches for mothers and infants." Infant Mental Health Journal. 2006. Vol 27; pp 327–43.

86. Illinois Academy of Family Physicians Maternal Depression and Child Development: strategies for primary care providers. Proceedings of the Family Practice Education Network Lisle, Illinois: Illinois Academy of Family Physicians, 2007.

87. Cox JL, Sagovsky R. "Detection of postnatal depression: development of the ten-item Edinburgh Postnatal Depression Scale." British Journal of Psychiatry. 1987. Vol 150; pp 782–6.

88. Moses-Kolko, et al. "Antepartum and postpartum depression: Healthy mom, healthy baby." Journal of the American Medical Association. 2004. Vol 59; pp 181–91.

89. Dietz PM, et al. "Clinically identified maternal depression before, during, and after pregnancies ending in live births." American Journal of Psychiatry. 2007. Vol 164 (10); pp 1515–20.

90. Oberlander T, et al. "Neonatal outcomes after prenatal exposure to selective serotonin reuptake inhibitor antidepressants and maternal depression using population-based linked health data." Arch Gen Psych. 2006. Vol 63; pp 898–906.

91. DiPietro J, et al. "Maternal psychological distress during pregnancy in relation to child development at age two." Child Dev. 2006. Vol 77; pp 573–87.

92. Chambers CD, et al. "Birth outcomes in pregnant women taking fluoxetine." N Engl J Med. 1996. Vol 335; pp 1010–5.

93. Kallen B, Otterblad Olausson P. "Antidepressant drugs during pregnancy and infant congenital heart defect." Reprod Toxicol. 2006. Vol 1; pp 221.

94. Lennestal R, Kallen B. "Discovery outcome in relationship to maternal use of some recently introduced antidepressants." J Clin Psychopharmacol. 2007. Vol 27; pp 607–13.

95. Oberlander T, et al. "Effects of timing and duration of gestational exposure to serotonin reuptake inhibitors: population based study." British J Psychiatry. 2008. Vol 192; pp 338–43.

96. Miller L. "Use of electroconvulsive therapy during pregnancy." Hosp Commun Psychiatry. 1994. Vol 45, No 5; pp 444–50.

97. Bennett HA, et al. "Depression during pregnancy: overview of clinical factors." Clin Drug Investig. 2004. Vol 24, No 3; pp 157–79.
Cohen LS, et al. "Relapse of major depression during pregnancy in women who maintain or discontinue antidepressant treatment. JAMA. 2006. Vol 295. No 5: 499–507.

98. McGrath C, Buist A, Norman TR. "Treatment of anxiety during pregnancy: effects of psychotropic drug treatment on the developing fetus." Drug Safety. 1999. Vol 20; pp 171–186.

99. Cohen LS, et al. "Course of panic disorder during pregnancy and the puerperium: a preliminary study." Biol Psychiatry. 1996. Vol 39; pp 950–954.

100. Regier, DA, et al. "The epidemiology of anxiety disorders: the epidemiologic catchment area (ECA) experience." J Psychiatr Res. 1990. Vol 2; pp 3–14.

101. Rizzardo R, et al. "Variations in anxiety levels during pregnancy and psychosocial factors in relation to obstetrical complication." Psychother Psychosom. 1988. Vol 49; pp 10–16.

102. Jeffries WS, Bochner F. "The effect of pregnancy on drug pharmacokinetics." Med J Aust. 1998. Vol 149; pp 675–677.

103. No authors listed. "Serotonin reuptake inhibitor antidepressants and pregnancy: many unanswered questions." Prescrire Int. 1999. Vol 43; pp 157–159.

104. Masand PS, Gupta S. "Selective serotonin reuptake inhibitors: an update." Harv Rev Psychiatry. 1999. Vol 7; pp 69–84.

105. Altshuler LL, et al. "Pharmacologic management of psychiatric illness during pregnancy: dilemmas and guidelines." Am J Psychiatry. 1996. Vol 153; pp 592–606.

106. Nordeng H, et al. "Neonatal withdrawal syndrome after in utero exposure to selective serotonin reuptake inhibitors." Acta Paediatr. 2001. Vol 90; pp 288–291.

107. Rementeria JL, Bhatt K. "Withdrawal symptoms on neonates from intra-uterine exposure to diazepam." J Pediatr. 1987. Vol 90; pp 123–126.

108. Cohen L, et al. "Birth outcomes following prenatal exposure to fluoxetine." Biol Psychiatry. 2000. Vol 48; pp 996–1000.

109. Laegreid L, et al. "Teratogenic effects of benzodiazepine use during pregnancy. J Pediatr. 1989. Vol 114; pp 126–131.

110. McNeil TF, et al. "Women with nonorganic psychosis: pregnancy's effect on mental health during pregnancy. Obstetric complications in schizophrenic patients." Acta Psychiatr Scand. 1984. Vol 70; pp 140–148.

111. Gentile S. "The clinical utilization of atypical antipsychotics in pregnancy and lactation." Ann Pharmacother. 2004. Vol 38; pp 1265–1271.

112. Altshuler L, et al. "Pharmacological management of psychiatric illness during pregnancy: dilemmas and guidelines." Am J Psychiatry. 1996. Vol 153; pp 592–596.

113. Australian Drug Evaluation Committee (ADEC) ADEC Pregnancy Category. http://www.tga.gov.au/DOCS/HTLM/medpreg.htm. Accessed 12/22/2015

114. Product Information. Abilify (aripiprazole) Princeton, NJ: Bristol-Myers Squibb; 2003.

115. Clozaril.® Prescribing information. http://www.pharma.us.novartis.com/product/pi/pdf/Clozaril.pdf. Accessed 12/22/2015/

116. Zyprexa. Prescribing information http://pi.lilly.com/us/zypreza-pi.pdf. Accessed 12/22/2015.

117. Goldstein DL, et al. "Olanzapine-exposed pregnancies and lactation: early experience." J Clin Psychopharmacol. 2000. Vol 20; pp 399–403.

118. Newport J, et al. "Atypical antipsychotic administration during late pregnancy: placental passage and obstetrical outcome." Am J Psychiatry. 2007. Vol 164; pp 1214–1220.

119. Klier CM, et al. "Pharmacokinetics and elimination of quetiapine, venlafaxine, and trazodone during pregnancy and postpartum." J Clin Psychopharmacol. 2007. Vol 27; pp 720–721.

120. Kruninger U, et al. "Pregnancy and lactation under treatment with quetiapine." Psychiatr Prax. 2007. Vol 34 (supplement); pp 75–76.

121. Risperdal (risperidone) Janssen, LP prescribing information. http://www.risperdal.com. Accessed 12/22/2015.

122. McCauley-Elsom K, et al. "Managing psychosis in pregnancy." Aust N Z J Psychiatry. 2007. Vol 41; pp 289–292.

123. Sertindole. Supportive material. http://www.serdolect.com/supportive_material/Default.aspx. Accessed 12/12/2015.

124. Geodon. Warning and precautions. http://www.rxlist.com/cgi/generic/ziprasidone_wcp.htm. Accessed 12/22/2015.

125. Seay PH, Field WE. "Toxicological studies on haloperidol." Int J Neuropsychiatry. 1968. Vol 3(supplement); pp 1–4.

126. Diav-Citrin O, et al. "Safety of haloperidol and penfluridol in pregnancy: a multicenter, prospective, controlled study." J Clin Psychiatry. 2005. Vol 66; pp 317–322.

127. Hansen LM, et al. "Haloperidol overdose during pregnancy." Obstet Gynecol. 1997. Vol 90; pp 659–661.

128. Bjarnason NH, et al. "Fetal exposure to pimozide: a case-report." J Reprod Med. 2006. Vol 51; pp 443–444.

129. Reis M, Kallen B. "Maternal use of antipsychotics in early pregnancy and delivery outcome." J Clin Psychopharmacol. 2008. Vol 28; pp 279–288.

130. Szabo KT, Brent RL. "Species differences in experimental teratogenesis by tranquilizing agents." Lancet. 1974. Vol 1; p 565.

131. Favre-Tissot M, Broussolle P. Du pouvoir teratogene éventuel des produits psychopharmacologique. In: Brill A, ed. Neuropsychopharmacology. Proceedings of the Fifth International Congress of the Collegium Internationale Neuro-psychopharmacologicum. Amsterdam, The Netherlands: Excepta Medica Foundation; 1967. pp 583–596.

132. Royal College of Obstetricians and Gynaecologists. The investigation and treatment of couples with recurrent miscarriage. Guidelines No. 17. http://www.rcog.org.uk/resources/Public/pdf/Recurrent_Miscarriage_No17.pdf. Accessed 12/22/2015.

133. Stika L, et al. "Effects of drug administration in pregnancy on children's school behavior." Pharm Weekbl Sci. 1990. Vol 12; pp 252–255.

134. Singh S, Padmanabdhan R. "Teratogenic effects of chlorpromazine hydrochloride in rat fetuses." Indian Med Res. 1978. Vol 67; pp 300–309.

135. Falterman CG, Richardson CJ. "Small left colon syndrome associated with maternal ingestion of psychotropic drugs." J Pediatr. 1980. Vol 97; pp 308–310.

136. Farag RA, et al. "Thanatrophic dwarfism associated with prochlorperazine administration." NY State J Med. 1978. Vol 78; pp 279–282.

137. Moriarty AJ, Nance MR. "Trifluoperazine and pregnancy." Can Med Assoc J. 1963. Vol 88; pp 375–376.

138. Canadian Department of National Health and Welfare, Food and Drug Directorate. Letter of notification to Canadian physicians. 1962. Ottawa, ON.

139. King JT, Barry MC, Neary ER. "Perinatal findings in women treated during pregnancy with oral fluphenazine." J New Drugs. 1963. Vol 3; pp 21–25.

140. Brougher JC. "The treatment of emotional disorders in obstetrics and gynecology with thioridazine." Q Rev Surg Obstet Gynecol. 1960. Vol 3; pp 44–47.

141. Vince DJ. "Congenital malformations following phenothiazine administration during pregnancy." Can Med Assoc J. 1969. Vol 100; p 223.

142. Mental Health Determinants and Populations Department of Mental Health and Substance Dependence. World Health Organization Geneva, 2000. Women's Mental Health: an evidence based review.

143. Pinkofsky HB, et al. "Psychotropic treatment during pregnancy." Am J Psychiatry. 1997. Vol 154; pp 718–719.

144. Goldstein DJ, et al. "Olanzapine-exposed pregnancies and lactation: early experience." J Clin Psychopharmacol. 2000. Vol 20; pp 399–403.

145. Coppola D, et al. "Evaluating postmarketing experience of risperidone use during pregnancy. Pregnancy and neonatal outcomes." Drug Saf. 2007. Vol 30; pp 247–64.

146. Newham JJ, et al. "Birth weight of infants after maternal exposure to typical and atypical antipsychotics: prospective comparison study." Br J Psychiatry. 2008. Vol 192; pp 333–337.

147. Council on drugs. Evaluation of a new antipsychotic agent. Haloperidol (Haldol) JAMA. 1968. Vol 205; pp 105–106.

148. Gentile S. "Managing suicidal risk in pregnant schizoaffective women." In: Murray WH, ed. Schizoaffective Disorder: New Research. 2nd ed.

149. Ladavac AS, et al. "Emergency management of agitation in pregnancy." Gen Hosp Psychiatry. 2007. Vol 29; pp 39–41.

150. Ellman LM, et al. "The effects of genetic liability for schizophrenia and maternal smoking during pregnancy on obstetric complications." Schizophr Res. 2007. Vol 93; pp 229–236.

151. Henin A, et al. "Psychopathology in the offspring of parents with bipolar disorder: a controlled study." Biol Psychiatry. 2005. Vol 58; pp 554–561.

152. Matthey S, et al. "Diagnosing postpartum depression in mothers and fathers: whatever happened to anxiety." J Affect Disord. 2003. Vol 74; pp 139–147.

153. Austin MP. "Antenatal screening and early intervention for 'perinatal distress', depression and anxiety. Where to from here?" Arch Women Ment Health. 2004. Vol 7; pp 1–6.

154. Milgrom J, Martin, PR, Negri LM. Treating postnatal depression: a psychological approach for health care practitioners. Chichester, John Wiley and Sons, 1999.

155. Emmanuel J, et al. "Systematic review of the outcome of anxiety and depressive disorders." Br J Psychiatry. 1998. Supplement 34(173); pp 35–41.

156. Ross LE, et al. "Measurement issues in postpartum depression part 1: anxiety as a feature of postpartum depression." Arch Women Ment Health. 2003. Vol 6; pp 51–57.

157. Terry DJ, Mayocchi L, Hynes GJ. "Depressive symptomatology in new mothers: a stress and coping perspective." J Abnormal Psychol. 1996. Vol 105; pp 220–231.

158. Boyce P, Stubbs J, Todd A. "The Edinburgh postnatal depression scale: validation for an Australian sample." Aust N Z J Psychiatry. 1993. Vol 27; pp 472–476.

159. Cox JL, Holden JM, Sagovsky R. "Detection of postnatal depression. Development of the 10-item Edinburgh Postnatal Depression Scale." Br J Psychiatry. 1987. Vol 150; pp 782–786.

160. Cox JL, et al. "Validation of the Edinburgh Postnatal Depression Scale (EPDS) in non-postnatal women." J Affect Disord. 1996. Vol 39; pp 185–189.

161. Dennis CL. "Can we identify mothers at risk for postpartum depression in the immediate postpartum period using the Edinburgh Postnatal Depression Scale?" J Affect Disord. 2004. Vol 78; pp 163–169.

162. Lovibond SH, Lovibond PF. Manual for the Depression Anxiety Stress Scales. 2nd Edition Sydney, Psychological Foundation of Australia 1995.

163. Brown TA, et al. "Psychometric properties of the depression anxiety stress scales (DASS) in clinical samples. Behav Res Ther. 1997. Vol 35; pp 79–89.

164. Johnson J, et al. "Service utilization and social morbidity associated with depressive symptoms in the community." JAMA. 1992. Vol 267; pp 1478–1483.

165. Miller RL, Pallant JF, Negri LM. "Anxiety and stress in the postpartum: is there more to postnatal distress than depression?" BMC Psychiatry. 2006. Vol 6; p 12.

166. Stuart S, et al. "Postpartum anxiety and depression: onset and comorbidity in a community sample." J Nerv Ment Disease. 1998. Vol 186, No 7; pp 420–424.

167. Kendell R, Chalmers J, Platz C. "Epidemiology of puerperal psychoses." Br J Psychiatry. 1987. Vol 150; p 662.

168. Wisner K, Peindl K, Hanusa B. "Symptomatology of affective and psychotic illnesses related to child-bearing." J Affective Disord. 1994. Vol 30; p 77.

169. Yonkers K, et al. "Management of bipolar disorder during pregnancy and the postpartum period." Am J Psychiatry. 2004. Vol 161; p 608.

170. Brockington IF. "Puerperal psychosis: motherhood and mental health." New York: Oxford University Press; 1996. p 200.

171. American Psychiatric Association. Diagnostic and statistical manual for mental disorders. 4. Washington, DC: American Psychiatric Press; 1994.

172. Viguera A, et al. "Risk of recurrence of bipolar disorder in pregnant and non-pregnant women." Am J Psychiatry. 2000. Vol 157; p 179.

173. Rahim FM, al-Sabiae. "A puerperal psychosis in a teaching hospital in Saudi Arabia; Clinical profile and cross-cultural comparison." Acta Psychiatr Scand. 1991. Vol 84; p 508.

174. CEMD. Confidential inquiries into maternal deaths: Why mothers die, 1997–99. London: Royal College of Obstetricians and Gynaecologists; 2001.

175. Kumar R, et al. "Clinical survey of a psychiatric mother and baby unit: characteristics of 100 consecutive admissions," J Affective Disord. 1995. Vol 33; p 11.

176. Seeman M. Gender differences in the prescribing of antipsychotic drugs." Am J Psychiatry. 2004. Vol 161; p 1324.

177. Resnick P. "Child murder by parents: a psychiatric review of filicide." Am J Psychiatry. 1969. Vol 126; p 325.

178. Jabs BE, et al. "Cycloid psychoses-from clinical concepts to biological foundations." J Neural Transm. 2002. Vol 109; p 907.

179. Pfuhlmann B, Stoeber G, et al. "Postpartum psychosis: prognosis, risk factors, and treatment." Curr Psychiatr Rep. 2002. Vol 4; p 185.

180. Hirschfeld R, et al. "Validity of the mood disorder questionnaire: a general population study." Am J Psychiatry. 2003. Vol 160; p 178.

181. Cohen LS. Massachusetts General Hospital: Handbook of general hospital psychiatry. 4. St. Louis: Mosby Yearbook; 1997.

182. Jaigobin C, Silver FL. "Stroke and pregnancy." Stroke. 2000. Vol 31; p 2948.

183. Wisner K, Peindl K, Hanusa B. "Psychiatric episodes in women with young children." J Affective Disord. 1995. Vol 34; p 1.

184. Agrawal P, Bhatia M, Malik S. "Postpartum psychosis; a study of indoor cases in general hospital psychiatric clinic." Acta Psychiatr Scand. 1990. Vol 81; p 571.

185. Vythilingham M, Chen J, Bremner JD. "Psychotic depression and mortality." Am J Psychiatry. 2003. Vol 160; p 574.

186. Wisner K, et al. "Obsessions and compulsions in women with postpartum depression." J Clin Psychiatry. 1999. Vol 60; p 176.

187. Brandes M, Soares CN, Cohen LS. "Postpartum onset obsessive-compulsive disorder: diagnosis and management." Arch Womens Ment Health. 2004. Vol 7; p 99.

188. Bosanac P, Buist A, Burrows G. "Motherhood and schizophrenic illness. A review of the literature." Aust NZ J Psychiatry. 2003. Vol 37; p 24.

189. Gonzalex-Pinto A, et al. "Psychoeducation and cognitive-behavioral therapy in bipolar disorder: an update." Acta Psychiatr Scand. 2004. Vol 109; p 83.

190. Cochran SD. "Preventing medical noncompliance in the outpatient treatment of bipolar affective disorders." J Consult Clin Psychol. 1984. Vol 52; p 873.

191. Zornberg G, Pope H. "Treatment of depression in bipolar disorder: new directions for research." J Clin Psychopharmacol. 1993. Vol 13; p 397.

192. Chaudron L, Jefferson J. "Mood stabilizers during breastfeeding: a review." J Clin Psychiatry. 2000. Vol 61; p 79.

193. Austin MPV. "Puerperal affective psychosis: is there a case for lithium prophylaxis?" Br J Psychiatry. 1992. Vol 161; p 692.

194. Ketter T, et al. "Metabolism and excretion of mood stabilizers and new anticonvulsants." Cell Mol Neurobiol. 1999. Vol 19; p 551.

195. Moretti ME, et al. "Monitoring lithium in breast milk: an individualized approach for breastfeeding mothers." The Drug Monitoring. 2003. Vol 25; p 364.

196. Kaplan PW. "Reproductive health effects and teratogenicity of antiepileptic drugs." Neurology. 2004. Vol 63 (Suppl 4); p S13.

197. Frey B, Schubiger G, Musy JP. "Transient cholestatic hepatitis in a neonate associated with carbamazepine exposure during pregnancy and breastfeeding." Eur J Pediatr. 1990. Vol 150; p 136.

198. Bulau P, Paar WD, von Unruh GE. "Pharmacokinetics of oxcarbazepine and 10-hydroxy-carbamazepine in the newborn child of an oxcarbazepine-treated mother." Eur J Clin Pharmacol. 1988. Vol 34; p 311.

199. Ketter T, et al. "Metabolism and excretion of mood stabilizers and new anticonvulsants." Cell Mol Neurobiol. 1999. Vol 19; p 511.

200. Kinon BJ, et al. "Hyperprolactinemia in response to antipsychotic drugs: characterization across comparative clinical trials." Psychoneuroendocrinology. 2003. Vol 28 (supplement 2); p 69.

201. Kirchheiner J, et al. "Healthy outcome under olanzapine treatment in a pregnant woman." Pharmacopsychiatry. 2000. Vol 33; p 78.

202. Protheroe C. "Pueperal psychosis: a long term study 1927–1961." Br J Psychiatry. 1969. Vol 111; p 9.

203. Reed P, Sermin N, Appleby L. "A comparison of clinical response to electroconvulsive therapy in puerperal and non-puerperal psychoses." J Affective Disord. 1999. Vol 54; p 255.

30.204. Ahokas A, et al. "Positive treatment effect of estradiol in postpartum psychosis: a pilot study." J Clin Psychiatry. 2000. Vol 61; p 166.

31.205. Rappa, L. Condensed Psychpharacology 2016: a pocket reference for psychiatry and psychiatric medications. Publisher RXPSYCH LLC, 83–84

32.206. McDorman MF, Rosenberg HM. "Trends in infant mortality by cause of death and other characteristics." Vital Health Stat. 1993. DHHS Publication PHS 94–1857.

33.207. Zopf PE Jr. Mortality Patterns and Trends in the United States. 1992. Westport, Conn: Greenwood Press.

34.208. Borra C, Iacuvou M, Sevilla A. "New evidence on breastfeeding and postpartum depression: the importance of understanding women's intentions." Maternal Child Health Journal. 2015. Vol 19; pp 897–907.

35.209. Thase ME, Friedman ES, Biggs MM, et al. "Cognitive therapy versus medication in augmentation and switch strategies as second-step treatments a STAR*D Report." J Am Psychiatry.2007. Vol 164: 739–752.

36.210. www.fda.gov/drugs/scienceresearch/researchareas/pharmacogenetics/ucmo83378.htm. Accessed February 12, 2016.

37.211.   www.chicagotribune.com. "Testing DNA to find best meds to fight Depression-Chicago." Chicago Tribune. August 28, 2015.

38.212.   https://genesight.com/pr-medicare. "Medicare for the first time to cover combinatorial genetic testing to guide individualized selection of depression medications. October 30, 2014.

39.213.   Serretti A, et al. "Meta-analysis of serotonin transporter gene promoter polymorphism (5-HTTLPR) association with selective serotonin reuptake inhibitor efficacy in depressed patients." Mol Psychiatry. 2007. Vol 12; pp 247–257.

40.214.   Horstmann, S, et al. "Pharmacogenomics of antidepressant drugs. Pharmacol Ther. 2009. Vol 124; pp 57–73.

41.215.   Porcelli S et al. "Pharmacogenetics of antidepressant response. J Psychiatry Neurosci. 2011. Vol 36; pp 87–113.

42.216.   Qin et al. "Effect of folic acid intervention on the change of serum folate level in hypertensive Chinese adults: do methylenetetrahydrofolate reductase and methionine synthase gene polymorphisms affect therapeutic responses?" Pharmacogenetics and Genomics. 2012. Vol 22; pp 421–428.

43.217.   Anderson CAM, et al. "Response of serum and blood cell folate concentrations to folic acid supplementation depends on methylenetetrahydrofolate reductase C677T: results from a crossover trial." Mol Nutr Food Res. 2013. Vol 57–644.

44.218.   Ashfield-Watt PAL, et al. "Methylenetetrahydrofolate reductase 677C>T genotype modulates homocysteine responses to a folate rich diet or low dose folic acid supplement: a randomized controlled trial. Am J Clin Nutr.2002. Vol 180–186.

Index

serotonin, 120–21, 159
serotonin norepinephrine reuptake
    inhibitors (SNRIs), 44, 131
sertindole, 61, 64, 182
sertraline, 15–16, 45, 119, 131, 141, 159
sleep deprivation, 107, 134–35, 139, 142
stillbirths, 10, 53, 56
stress, 10, 37–38, 42, 99, 101, 107, 114, 124,
    126–29, 184–85
substance abuse, 6, 11–12, 74, 177, 179
Substance Abuse and Mental Health
    Services Administration, 77, 177
suicide, 12, 23, 26, 36, 43, 53, 67, 101, 124,
    135
symptoms, 11, 20–21, 26, 34–35, 53–54,
    78–79, 99–102, 117–18, 134–45,
    161–62
  depressive, 12–13, 18–19, 50, 110–11,
    124, 152, 154–55, 178, 185
  extrapyramidal, 45, 63
  psychological, 41, 71
  psychotic, 21, 64, 67, 136, 142, 148, 162
  withdrawal, 30, 45–47, 66, 73, 76–78,
    162, 175, 181
syndromes, 5, 10, 16, 45, 53, 56, 72–73,
    77–79, 94–95, 145–47
  discontinuation, 45
  fetal alcohol, 10
  floppy infant, 65
  infant death, 53, 56, 94
  jittery baby, 16, 81
  metabolic, 147
  neonatal abstinence, 72, 76–79, 173,
    177–78
  neonatal withdrawal, 162
  perinatal, 5, 45
  polycystic ovarian, 145
  respiratory distress, 94–95
  Stevens-Johnson, 146

T

Tegretol. *See* carbamazepine
therapies, 28, 40–41, 47, 101, 115, 119, 132,
    142, 159
  alternative, 119, 159

antidepressant, 2, 12–13, 21, 106
antipsychotic, 64, 67
cognitive behavioral, 41, 50, 101, 114,
    132, 141–42, 162
electroconvulsive (ECT), 21, 31–32, 53,
    118, 140, 148, 162, 181, 187
light, 12, 119
nonpharmacologic, 162
reproductive, 40
thioridazine. *See* phenothiazines
trifluoperazine, 57, 63

U

United States Preventative Services Task
    Force (USPSTF), 2, 80–81
utero exposure, 63, 65–66, 173, 181

V

valproate, 30, 131, 139, 145–46
valproic acid, 27–30, 131, 139, 145, 156,
    176
venlafaxine, 16, 19, 45, 120, 131, 182

W

Wellbutrin. *See* bupropion

Z

ziprasidone, 27–28, 31, 61, 64–65, 139, 147,
    155
zolpidem, 42
Zyprexa. *See* olanzapine

Printed in the United States
By Bookmasters